T0146826

The Impending Great Tribulation Apocalypse

Mike Penrod

authorHOUSE®

AuthorHouse™
1663 Liberty Drive
Bloomington, IN 47403
www.authorhouse.com
Phone: 1 (800) 839-8640

Illustrations Coordinator: Rosalie White
Illustrator: Stephen Adams
Colorist: Brian Mumphrey

Published by AuthorHouse 05/30/2017

ISBN: 978-1-5246-1520-8 (sc)
ISBN: 978-1-5246-1519-2 (e)

Library of Congress Control Number: 2016910171

Print information available on the last page.

Many thanks to Michael McAuley, Lois Crum, Ken Cuffey, Jordan, Matt and Greg Moore for their help. Additional thanks to Amber, Rosalie, and Steve at Author House for their help.

The version of the Bible will be noted after every quote, to give credit where credit is due. Many verse numbers have been maintained for quick reference. "EM" notes that emphasis is mine. Some italic is from the NASB.

The art work on the back cover is owned by Mike Penrod. This art work of two horses with barding is by Jason Profant.

Contact aerosol317@aol.com.

Contents

A Perspective of Matthew 24 to Revelations Chapters 1-8. The Context.
The Third Parallel View

Acknowledgments

My intention in writing this book is to show God's creativity—God who created such an interesting puzzle, overlooked by many of us.

Thanks to my wife, who is so very forbearing. Thanks to my mother and father, who maintained such a loving and balanced Christian life.

I hope that what God has done will give you some exciting insight you have searched for, and understanding of the end times. I hope to see you in the clouds! Don't try to take any baggage. If you are taking a shower when the rapture occurs, don't worry; you will likely be wearing a robe in the twinkling of an eye.

Best wishes in Christ,

Mike

1 Grounding Thoughts

I am not claiming that we can know the exact date the Great Tribulation will start. I do think that, following the clues in the Bible and using a bit of conjecture, suggests it is almost certain that the Great Tribulation will start before 2027. Yes, many people have made such statements, and many have obviously been wrong. I may be added to that list. At the least, I think you will be intrigued by the evidence. Since I cannot see the future, I cannot tell you what actions you should or should not take. I have offered a few ideas for your consideration; however, the decisions are yours to make.

This book does not investigate in any depth the events that will occur during the last half of the Great Tribulation. The timing of its start, the rapture, and related events that help reveal the timing are important enough to focus on almost exclusively. If you think there is something in Scripture that says we can't know the *general* time, you might want to reread that passage again very carefully—or read on.

Why is the timing important? If you have friends or family members who have not accepted Christ as their Lord, you may have very little time to help guide them to Christ. There may also be secondary things you will wish to rethink.

"When there are many words, transgression is unavoidable, …" (Prov. 10:19, NASB). Therefore beware. There must be a number of errors to be found, even in a book as brief as this one. However, the overall concept seems to resolve many conflicts between pre-tribulation, mid-tribulation, and post-tribulation views, leading to a harmony of passages. Therefore it is difficult to imagine that the concept itself is wrong in general.

The concept presented is not easy for everyone to understand. Therefore I have used more than one method (simple, somewhat detailed, and visual) to communicate what God has done in the verses focused on. The book is intended to be as much a study as a story. Therefore some of conventions of formatting have been disregarded, to hopefully aid understanding by visualization and for purposes of reference.

We could become rich if we knew the future. We now have an opportunity, knowing what lies ahead, to make a spiritual investment. Think wisely in regard to what God has done, as it may give you insight about what is soon to come. No man created this information. God created the information through others long ago. He has fortunately given us understanding of some of these writings.

Most of the biblical quotations are from the New American Standard Version (NASB), and a few are from the King James Version (KJV). Aside from some italics, all emphasis (**bold**, *italics*, [], or underline) has been added by myself and noted "EM" (emphasis mine).

My discussion is directed primarily to Christians, since those who do not believe in the God of the Bible will likely consider the Biblical Apocalypse to be myth. If you have not made a commitment to Christ, I hope you will find the parallel and the improbability of events that have already occurred to be of interest.

2   Defying Scripture?

Some people seem to be upset with the use of the word *rapture*, since it is not used in the Bible. This should not be of consequence. It is simply a word coined to refer to the phrase "shall be caught up," used in 1 Thessalonians 4:16–17 "For the Lord Himself will descend from heaven with a shout, with the voice of the archangel, and with the trumpet of God; and the dead in Christ shall rise first. 17 Then we who are alive and remain ***shall be caught up*** together with them in the clouds to meet the Lord in the air, and thus we shall always be with the Lord" (NASB, EM). Please beam us up Lord, soon!

"But know this first of all, that no prophecy of Scripture is a matter of one's own interpretation" (2 Pet. 1:20, NASB). Many of you reading are more knowledgeable about end-time prophecy and have more insight than I do. Therefore, you might think some of the ideas expressed here are interpretation. If what has seemed to be conflict between various verses is resolved, please be cautious about rejecting the concept.

For anyone not familiar with the terms, here are some brief definitions. *Pre-tribulation* rapture means that God will take Christians out of the world before the suffering of the Great Tribulation. *Mid-tribulation* means that God will take Christians out of the world amid the Great Tribulation suffering. *Post-tribulation* refers to Christians being taken as the great suffering ends.

3 You Can't Know When The Great Tribulation-Apocalypse or the Rapture Will Occur?

Numerous people have given dates for the apocalypse and the Second Coming, and yet these events have not occurred. Many would say it is crazy or a big mistake to think that we can know even approximately when the rapture will occur. On the other hand, if you find something amazing that leads to great insight, you may gain confidence in what appears to be a wager.

"Surely the lord God does nothing unless He reveals His secret counsel to His servants the prophets." (Amos 3:7, NASB). If God tells His prophets what He is doing, then we just might find what is recorded regarding our time.

"…understand that the vision pertains to the time of the end." (Dan. 8:17, NASB). "…seal up the book until the end of time; …" (Dan. 12:4, NASB). Based on these passages, the book will be unsealed at some time. Which could lead to knowing a close timing of Christ's return?

The prophets were given a message; let us hope we can understand it even in part. Thankfully, God has been revealing—unsealing—what He is doing, some to one man, a bit to another. There are numerous writers, such as Hal Lindsay, John Haggey, Rabi Jonathan Cahn and Perry Stone, who have been given understanding of some of the events that have been happening even today. Thanks to these men and others, and to God, who has worked through them.

In regard to Christ's return:

"But of that <u>day</u> and <u>hour</u> no one knows, …" (Matt. 24:36, NASB, EM).

"Therefore be on the alert, for you do not know which <u>day</u> your Lord is coming." (Matt. 24:42, NASB, EM).

"For this reason you be ready too; for the Son of Man is coming at an <u>hour</u> when you do not think He will." (Matt. 24:44, NASB, EM).

"the master of that slave will come on a <u>day</u> when he does not expect *him* and at an <u>hour</u> which he does not know, …" (Matt. 24:50, NASB, EM).

Jesus said it; it is true. Unfortunately, these passages are frequently quoted out of the context of the book and chapter they come from. Before Matthew 24:50 which was just quoted was the context. "But if that <u>evil</u> slave says in his heart, 'My master is not coming for a long time,' 49 and shall begin to beat his fellow slaves and eat and drink with drunkards; 50 the master of <u>that</u> slave will come on a day when <u>he</u> does not expect *him* and an hour which <u>he</u> does not know." (Matt. 24:48-50, NASB, EM) This passage is intended for the evil slave, almost certainly speaking of those who never except Christ.

Christ also said in Matthew 5:18–19, "For truly I say to you, until heaven and earth pass away, not the smallest letter or stroke shall pass away from the Law, until all is accomplished.19 "Whoever then annuls one of the least of these commandments, and so teaches others, shall be called least in the kingdom of heaven; …" (NASB).

Should we assume that Jesus was generalizing when He said, "But of that day and hour no one knows" (NASB)? We could say that Jesus's statement meant we could have no idea of the time He would return. But we should be very careful not to assume too much. There is a high probability that Jesus literally meant, "But of that **day and hour** no one knows" (NASB, EM). To generalize could be adding to Christ's statement.

Jesus said, "You blind guides, who strain out a gnat and swallow a camel!" (Matt. 23:24, NASB). Jesus was criticizing the scribes and Pharisees for focusing on the less important, which caused them to miss the big picture, that of greatest importance.

What could we miss out on by assuming that "day and hour" means we cannot have any idea when Christ will come? "Now as to the times and the epochs, brethren, you have no need of anything to be written to you. 2 For you yourselves know full well that the day of the Lord will come just like a thief in the night. 3 While **they** are saying, "Peace and safety!" then destruction will come upon **them** suddenly like birth pangs upon a woman with child; and **they** shall not escape. 4 **But you, brethren, are not in darkness, that the _day_ should overtake you like a _thief_,**" (1 Thess. 5:1–4, NASB, EM).

Knowing that the day spoken of will come, yet saying we can have no idea when, could mean that it will *overtake* Christians by surprise. "Yes, we knew it was coming, but we didn't know it was coming!" This passage from 1 Thessalonians says we should know. Scripture gives us enough information about the general time period that the day should not take us by surprise.

"Do not be excessively righteous, and do not be overly wise. Why should you ruin yourself?" (Eccles. 7:16, NASB). Some Christians seem to be upset with this passage, as it appears at odds with another command in the Bible, " ...thus you shall be holy for I am holy,'" (Lev. 11:45, NASB).

Will we focus so hard on not jaywalking that we end up cursing God, gossiping, stealing, and lying? Or search out every trite detail with wisdom to such excessive depth of thought that it drives us to insanity and wastes time that could be better spent on more important priorities? Or possibly take pride in the thought that we are holy, when in fact we have over looked our horrendous sin?

Solomon's statement in Ecclesiastes 7:16 sounds like Christ's statement in Matthew 23:24, where Jesus speaks of straining at a gnat and then swallowing a camel. The point in both cases is almost certainly that we should not become so focused on less significant points that we miss the big picture, which includes being sure the thought is in context.

Jesus - "You hypocrites! You know how to analyze the appearance of the earth and the sky, but why do you not analyze this present time?" (Luke 12:56, NASB). "And in the morning, '*There will be* a storm today, for the sky is red and threatening.' Do you know how to discern the appearance of the sky, but cannot *discern* the signs of the times? 4 "An evil and adulterous generation seeks after a sign; and a sign will not be given it, except the sign of Jonah." (Matt.16:3-4, NASB). Does this apply to us today? Jesus was saying the teachers of the day should have been able to understand the evil of the day and perhaps the time of Christ's first coming from prophecy. Christ also mentioned the sign for that time period, His death and resurrection. In Matt. 3:13-17 John the Baptist is open minded, and seems convinced, that Jesus is the Messiah. John, like many, likely thought that Jesus was going to be the reigning King, yet Jesus was not ruling, nor let John out of prison. John likely had second thoughts. Is Jesus not the Christ? In Matt. 11:4&5 Jesus sends word to John. Blindness is healed, some dead arise and He has preached good news to the poor. These are evidence, signs that Jesus was the Messiah, yet not a raising of one's self from the dead, nor opening the sky to see a heavenly Kingdom, the type of sign the Pharisees seemed to demand. Faith is not by sight. Two types of signs?

In the opening verses of Matthew 24, Jesus' disciples ask "when" and about "the sign" of Christ's return. Jesus then spends all of Matthew 24 and 25 answering when this will be, explaining how to recognize the time, and teaching the most important way in which we should respond— spiritually—in our relationship with God. There is no passage in Matthew 24 in which Jesus says He will not give His disciples a sign, which they ask for.

Why would Jesus use twenty-eight verses telling us when "these things" will occur and speaking of "the sign" if we could not have any idea when these things are going to happen? If that were the case, Jesus could just have said, "It's going to be a surprise, guys."

Four verses before Jesus says we can't know the day or the hour, He says, "Now learn the parable from the fig tree: **when** its branch has already become tender, and puts forth its leaves, **you <u>know</u> that <u>summer is near</u>;** 33 even so **you too, when you see all these things, <u>recognize</u> that He is near, right at the door."** (Matt. 24:32–33, NASB, EM). Jesus mentions a time period: when you see these things. How close will it be when you see these things? "recognize", "know", it is "right at the door."

Jesus is describing a specific time period of His return, though he also says you can't know the day or hour. People have read this passage over and over and have seemingly become frustrated by false anticipation or lack of understanding. Yet this does not change Christ's statement that when you see these things, you can "know."

Christ also talked about "when … summer is near" (NASB). When summer comes, things get heated up; almost everything is in full bloom and bears fruit. Jesus is almost certainly speaking of a specific time, which is like a season. Not a day, not an hour, yet a specific time period that is recognizable. As Jesus stated, you can "recognize" and "know" "when you see <u>all</u> these things."

"Then the devil took Him into the holy city; and he had Him stand on the pinnacle of the temple, 6 and said to Him, "If You are the Son of God throw Yourself down; for it is written, 'HE WILL GIVE HIS ANGELS CHARGE CONCERNING YOU'; and 'On *their* HANDS THEY WILL BEAR YOU UP, LEST YOU STRIKE YOUR FOOT AGAINST A STONE.'" 7 Jesus said to him, "On the other hand, it is written, 'YOU SHALL NOT PUT THE LORD YOUR GOD TO THE TEST.'" (Matthew 4:5–7, NASB).

We have heard many times, "But of that day and hour no one knows, …" (Matt. 24:36, NASB), yet the quotation is frequently taken out of context. People rarely mention that Jesus also said "recognize" and "know." Change a phrase slightly and the meaning can become distorted, no longer meaning what was intended. What "the devil" did intentionally in Matthew 4:5, using Scripture out of context, we can do by mistake.

"The Feast of Trumpets happens on the 'new moon,' which is 29.5 days after the last one, meaning it might occur on the 29th or 30th day, nobody knows for sure. 'Of that day or hour no one knows' is an expression referring to this feast, and thus, the rapture."

"'Of that day or hour no man knows, but my Father only' is an expression used by a groom when asked when his wedding will be. He says this because it is his Father that will tell him when his preparation on the bridal chamber are completed and it is time. Again the wedding pictures the rapture." www.bibleprophesy.org/introtrumpets.htm 5/9/2016 Bible Prophesy.org Jason Hammel

Christ's use of the phrase "of the day or hour no one knows" does not seem to be a general statement that we could have no idea when He would return. Jesus was likley referring to Yom Teruah – Rosh Hashanah – the Feast of Trumpets. The Feast of Trumpets has not had its prophetic fulfillment. Christ is likely stating His return for the rapture of Christians will take place during the Feast of Trumpets and no one will know if this will occur on the first or second day of the Feast, nor the hour.

"September 25th is also known as Yom Teruah, the Feast of Trumpts. Observed on the First and Second of Tishri, the celebration actually begins 29 days earlier: a series of over 90 trumpet blasts accrue for a final blowing of blasts on the climax of the celebration, the Teki'ah Gedolah, the Great Blowing. . . .the last, climactic blast, the Teki'at Shofar . . . This is not the usual series of short bursts, signaling alarm or bad news. Rather, it is a long blast, signaling victory or good news. It is this last blast that is referred to as the last trump." Chuck Missler www.Khouse.org/articles/1995/105/ 5/9/2016

"in a moment, in the twinkling of an eye, at the last trumpet; for the trumpet will sound, and the dead will be raised imperishable, and we shall be changed." I Cor. 15:52 This is the rapture with a trumpet.

"Your dead will live; their corpses will rise, you who lie in the dust, awake and shout for joy, for your dew is as the dew of the dawn, and the earth will give birth to the departed spirits." (Isaiah 26:19). "It will come about also in that day that a great trumpet will be blown;" (Isaiah 26:13, NASB). The rapture again mentioned with a trumpet.

Just after mentioning "of that day and hour no one knows," Jesus mentions "the coming of the Son of Man" in Matthew 24:27, the timing of which is almost certainly explained by the Feast of Trumpets.

"Now having been questioned by the Pharisees as to when the kingdom of God was coming, He answered them and said, "The kingdom of God is not coming with signs to be observed; 21 nor will they say, 'Look, here it is!' or, 'There it is!' For behold, the kingdom of God is in your midst." (Luke 17:20-21, NASB)

In Luke 17:20-21 Jesus seems to be clear that He was there so the kingdom of God was there. In the past, the star of Bethlehem had been seen which seems to clearly have been a sign of Jesus arrival. The Pharisees must have been looking for a more miraculous sign.

"And there will be signs in sun and moon and stars, and upon the earth dismay among the nations, in perplexity at the roaring of the sea and the waves," (Luke 21:25 NASB)

Like the star of Bethlehem which may have been a rare alignment of planets, these signs will not necessarily be miraculous in the way the Pharisees demanded, yet they will still be rare events and therefore overlooked by many.

You can explain the Cosmological Fine Tuning to people. You can explain the many things that must be precisely as they are, some beyond astronomical probability in our known universe, for there to be life. For examples, see Hugh Ross's book *The Creator and the Cosmos,* Gerald L. Schroeder's *The Science of God,* and Peter D. Ward and Donald Brownlee's *Rare Earth.*[1]

You can talk to people about our DNA being poly-functional, and therefore poly-constrained, implying or proving that our DNA is in a state of entropy (that is, not evolving, but deteriorating more and more). This information can be found in Dr. J. C. Sanford's book *Genetic Entropy & The Mystery of the Genome.*[2] Dr. Sanford explains the degradation of the human genome.

You can mention the extreme improbability that the simplest microorganism would form by chance—that is, the chance of 150 amino acids bonding together correctly to form a functional protein. Numerous other amino acids would likewise have to form other functional proteins to then bond together correctly to form an extremely simple microorganism. For this to occur by chance is shockingly improbable to any comparison of our known universe. Stephen Meyer explains in his book *Signature in the Cell.*[3]

Some of the foremost scientists now think that aliens may have created life and seeded it on earth. What happened to the scientific faith that life evolved on earth in a primordial soup?

Yet with all of this formidable evidence of great improbability that life could arise by chance, it does not seem to cause most people to consider the likelihood that there is a God. How could they then even consider a biblical Apocalypse?

Our time is just as Jesus described: "For the coming of the Son of Man will be just like the days of Noah. 38" For as in those days which were before the flood **they** were eating and drinking, **they** were marrying and giving in marriage, until the day that Noah entered the ark, 39 and **they** did not understand until the flood came …" (Matt. 24:37–39, NASB, EM). "*They*" refers to non-Christians. The people of Noah's day, who lived near him, surely saw how Noah lived his life, and Noah surely talked to them about God. "But you, brethren, are not in darkness, that the day should overtake you like a thief;" (1 Thess. 5:4, NASB).

The entire chapter of Matthew 24 was triggered by four questions asked by Jesus's disciples: "And as He was sitting on the Mount of Olives, the disciples came to Him privately, saying, "… Tell us, <u>when</u> will these <u>things</u> be, and <u>what</u> will be the of <u>sign of Your coming</u>, and of the <u>end of the age</u>?"

(Matt. 24:3, NASB, EM). If we could not have any idea of when Christ would return, why would Jesus bother with a lengthy answer? It would be pointless. He could simply have said, "No one knows," but He didn't.

Recognizing that we can't know whether Christ will return on Tuesday at 10:00 a.m. or Wednesday at 11:30 p.m. won't cause any greater problem than we already face. In fact, the Bible may give the time of Christ's return within approximately six weeks, or two days from a specific event.

Christ's responses to knowing "when" and the "sign" can be compared to a time-limited bank safe. Specific things must occur during a specific time, some in a specific order. In Matthew 24:33, Jesus said, "**when** you see all these things." (NASB, EM)

There is one more reason some people may strongly oppose the idea of knowing even a general time frame for the Great Tribulation, sometimes called the Apocalypse. When people are faced with the reality, that an extremely horrific situation might have to be experienced, it can be more than some people's minds can cope with.

In such cases, *denial* is a mental coping mechanism. People say they refuse to believe it, though they think, on some level, that it might be true. Even your suggestion of such an event might cause them to accuse you of being fearful, hoping you will stop talking about it, which in turn may take their minds off of the subject. Another reason for disbelief.

If someone thinks you don't believe a horrific event is coming, then that person may feel more confident that the event will not occur. Of course, it may be difficult to determine if this is their thinking.

It is also possible that some atheists spend most of their lives working to find evidence that will convince others that there is no God, in an attempt to assure themselves that there is no God.

When will these things occur? The suggested answer starts in just a few pages.

4   A Jigsaw Puzzle

If a jigsaw puzzle manufacturer produces a quality puzzle, no two pieces will be exactly the same shape. In that way the intended picture will be revealed when all the pieces are properly placed. Trying to force pieces into place results in bent and folded puzzle pieces, with some gaps and an unclear picture.

This is what we have had in the conflict between a pre-tribulation rapture, a mid-tribulation rapture, and a post-tribulation rapture. Most of the explanations end with what others consider to be conflicts with other Biblical concepts. If this is the case, we have not understood one passage or another correctly. Yes, this assumes that the Bible is inerrant—no flaws to be found if we understand it. That is the presupposition. A fresh view of some words, phrases, and chapter associations should make the puzzle fit together, creating a clear picture, though just a bit complex.

There are some things we learned long ago and have heard over and over again, anchoring these ideas in our brains even when they are wrong. The biblical view being presented here is made even more difficult to understand when concepts learned long ago are wrong.

The primary difficulty is the amount of information condensed in these chapters. More than one event is timed. In one of the chapters, some events discussed are not in obvious consecutive order. It may require reading the chapters a few times before the main idea falls into place. Hopefully you can enjoy what God has done.

5   Coming of Age: The "Last Days" Overall Time Period

Jesus was answering the disciples' question, "When will these things be?" (Matt. 24:3, NASB). During his explanation Jesus mentioned Daniel in Matthew 24:15, which infers that Daniel was writing about the same subject. (Daniel 12:4 KJV): "But thou, O Daniel, shut up the words, and seal the book, *even* to the **time of the end; ...**" In Matthew 24:3 Jesus' disciples ask, "... what will be the sign of Your coming, and of **the end of the age?**" (NASB, EM). Daniel mentions, not the end of time itself, but the end of a time period. This seems to be supported by the disciples' question about the end of the age and no mention by Jesus of the end of time. "But thou, O Daniel, shut up the words, and seal the book, *even* to the time of the end: <u>many shall run to and fro</u>, ..." (Daniel 12:4, KJV, EM).

If we had a time machine that could bring people from five thousand years ago up through the 1800s into the future, they would almost certainly be shocked. Common transportation would have been horses, donkeys and sailboats until the 1800s, when steamships and steam trains were more common. During World War I, travelers would see steel ships, tanks, biplanes, and trucks. In the 1930s–1940s they would see automobiles become affordable and widespread. In the 1970s, jet airplanes became more common to the masses for commercial transportation. The sight of all this rapid transportation would likely cause the time traveler to think of people rushing to and fro. The time period Daniel spoke of likely started about 1914, during World War I.

"But thou, O Daniel, shut up the words and seal the book, *even* to the time of the end: many shall run to and fro, **and knowledge shall be increased.**" (Dan. 12:4, KJV, EM). In the 1970s, the personal computer started to become a part of people's lives. About the mid-1990s, the Internet became available to many people. With computers and the Internet, information started to become readily available to much of the population of the earth. This was the birth of the Information Age, at which time the statement "**knowledge shall be increased**" (KJV, EM) was fulfilled. Just as most people in the Stone Age made great use of stone, those in the Bronze Age made use of bronze, and those in the Iron Age made use of iron, so the wide use of information is the hallmark of the Information Age.

> Credit to Hal Lindsey who noticed Daniel's reference to two age distinguishing events which are being addressed. "We are told in Daniel 12 how prophecy "will not be understood until the end times, when travel and education shall be vastly increased." THE LATE GREAT PLANET EARTH. [1]

"Many shall run to and fro" (KJV) almost certainly describes the latter part of the Industrial Age, and "knowledge shall be increased" (KJV) almost certainly describes the Information Age. These are mentioned in Daniel 12:4 in the same order as their occurrence in historical time.

There is no mention of another age between the Industrial Age and the Information Age. If another age had occurred between these two ages, it would create doubt that these two ages were the ones being spoken of. In addition, there has yet to be the start of a new age, such as an "Artificial Intelligence Age" or an "Atomic Printing Age." This seems further confirmation as another age is not mentioned. It would not be too surprising to see some androids with artificial intelligence or computers that are self-aware, yet not common, before the rapture.

This gives us four reasons to think that the Industrial Age and the Information Age are the time periods being spoken of in Daniel 12:4. To fit together like a puzzle, other prophecies must fit the Daniel 12:4 passage; otherwise there must be a mistake. This is the first passage that gives us reason to believe we have been living in the time period spoken of as "the last days" or "the end of the age." The Industrial Age is past; we are now living in the Information Age.

"I found Israel like grapes in the wilderness; I saw your forefathers as the earliest fruit on the fig tree in its first season. …" (Hosea 9:10, NASB). In this passage, God is making a comparison between Israel and the Jews as precious fruit, a fig tree, valued in His eyes. Hal Lindsey was likely the first to note this passage and its importance.[2] Jesus uses the same image: "Now learn the parable from the fig tree: when its branch has already become tender, and puts forth its leaves ..." (Matt. 24:32, NASB). In the fall, deciduous trees lose their leaves. They appear to be dead. In fact, in most cases you cannot tell, by appearance, which non-evergreen trees are dead in winter and which are still alive.

God says of his people, "Also I swore to them in the wilderness that I would scatter them among the nations and disperse them among the lands, 24 because they had not observed My ordinances, but had rejected My statutes, and had profaned My Sabbaths, and their eyes were on the idols of their fathers." (Ezek. 20:23–24, NASB).

More confirmation that God foretold that His people would be scattered into the nations is found in Hosea 9:17 "My God will cast them away because they have not listened to Him; and they will be wanderers among the nations." (NASB). There are more references, enough that it appears God did not want us to miss this point. (See Jer. 9:16, 16:15; Lam. 1:3, 4:15–16, 20; Ezek. 11:16–17, 12:15, 22:15; Zech. 10:9; Hosea 8:8.) Still today we can see that some Jews are scattered among the nations. They peacefully live among us here in America. Unfortunately, there has been a recent uptick in the hate marches against Jews, one of which occurred in Germany a few years ago. Some things don't seem to change.

God has more to say. "'In those days and at that time,' declares the Lord, 'search will be made for the iniquity of Israel, but there will be none; and for the sins of Judah, but they will not be found; for I shall pardon those whom I leave as a remnant.'" (Jer. 50:20, NASB) (also see Ezek. 6:8). There has always been a small remnant of Jews living in Israel, though often hardly enough to be called a nation. Nonetheless, some always remained.

"and said to Jeremiah the prophet, "Please let our petition come before you, and pray for us to the Lord your God, that is for all this remnant; because we are left but a few out of many, as your own eyes can see us," (Jer. 42:2, NASB). Despite a small population of Jews, the San Remo resolution of April 25, 1920, recognized Israel as the nation of the Jews. If no Jews had been living in Israel at the time, it would have been absurd to have confirmed Israel as the nation of the Jews. Even for those of us not alive at that time, the San Remo resolution confirms Israel as the nation of the Jews.

God has more to say. "The Lord God, who gathers the dispersed of Israel, declares, "Yet others I will gather to them, to those already gathered." (Isa. 56:8, NASB). There are many more verses confirming the same statement. (See Isa. 43:5–6; Jer. 16:15–16, 29:14,18, 23:3, 31:7–8, 32:37; Ezek. 11:17, 20:41–42, 28:25, 34:13, 36:24, 37:21, 39:27–28; Zech. 10:10.)

During World War II, Jews suffered greatly in German concentration camps, were burned to death in gas chambers and also suffered in other parts of the world. Seeking safety, a large number of Jews boarded ships and headed to Israel after the war. On May 14, 1948, Jews disembarked from ships, and "the fig tree"—Israel—came to life. Its "branch" had "become tender" (NASB). Israel was as new as a young branch, as God said it would be.

God made an even more precise statement in Isaiah 66:8: "Who has heard such a thing? Who has seen such things? Can a land be born in one day? Can a nation be brought forth all at once? ..." (NASB). Jews returned to Israel and then disembarked in one day. Not only did Jesus say it would occur, God said Israel would be born in one day. This sounds as much like being reborn as being born. In either case it was very unlikely, and yet it occurred.

Israel being born or reborn sounds almost like a parallel with John 3:3: "Jesus answered and said to him, 'Truly, truly, I say to you, **unless one is born again**, he cannot see the kingdom of God." (NASB, EM). Does this in any way relate to Israel's establishment in 1948? In Ezekiel 20:23-24, God said He would scatter Israel among the nations because they did not obey and did not observe His ordinances, which is sin. "And you were dead in your trespasses and sins," (Eph. 2:1, NASB). Could it be that Israel, as a nation, had been dead to God due to its sin and was given new life?

Is this an allegory? A nation, a people, in some way born in one day, as we who accept Christ are born again? A physical nation, a nation of such small stature as to not be alive, also a spiritual nation, born in one day?

Jesus used the fig tree to speak of Israel, then figuratively explained that this previously existing country would be born—come to life. "Now learn the parable from the fig tree; when its branch has already become tender, and puts forth its leaves, **you <u>know</u> that <u>summer is near</u>; 33 even so you too, when you see all these things, <u>recognize </u>that He is <u>near, right at the door</u>."** (Matt. 24:32–33, NASB, EM). The words "know" and "recognize" let us understand that we can have confidence that Jesus's return is close when Israel is reborn.

> "Truly I say to you, **this generation will not pass away until all these things take place.**" (Matt. 24:34, NASB, EM). Hal Lindsey has given a very helpful insight. Hal Lindsey realized that if we know when Israel was born— 1948—and also know how many years are in a generation, the span of a generation can be added to 1948, and that should tell us the approximate time by which Christ will return. *Approximate* as in a general season, not the day or the hour. How long is a generation? Hal Lindsay "What generation? Obviously, in context, the generation that would see the signs—chief among them the rebirth of Israel. A generation in the Bible is something like forty years. If this is a correct deduction, then within forty years or so of 1948 all these things could take place."[2]

Hal Lindsey was also very wise in saying, "If this is a correct deduction." He did not say he absolutely knew, nor did he say he had heard the voice of God. He did not claim to be a prophet. He said "could take place," as in *might* take place.

If we add 40 to 1948, we come up with approximately 1988. This sounds logical. People living approximately two thousand years ago, without contemporary medicine, might only have lived to be about forty years old. Many American settlers did not live to forty.

The year 1988 came and went without the rapture or the Great Tribulation. Therefore, as reasonable as Hal's time frame was, it missed. Mr. Lindsey doesn't miss much. In fact, the Information Age started within the time period he suggested. We can read and read the Bible and still miss things. Is there any passage in the Bible that might define a Biblical generation?

There are only a few, perhaps just two. "Then the Lord said, 'My spirit shall not strive with man forever, because he also is flesh; nevertheless his days shall be one hundred and twenty years.'" (Gen. 6:3, NASB). Prior to this verse, Methuselah is mentioned: "So all the days of Methuselah were nine hundred sixty-nine years, and he died." (Gen. 5:27, NASB). Afterward, God sets an approximate limit on the human life span of 120 years. Approximately only 20 or 30 people are then noted in the Bible to have lived more than 120 years after the Genesis 6:3 statement.

The number 120 does not seem to be a reference to a generation, but a limit or very close limit of the human life span. In the 1970s, scientists found a structure on the end of the human chromosome called a *telomere*. The telomere protects a chromosome from unraveling. The telomere has been compared to the plastic tip on the end of a shoelace. If that plastic tip wears away, the shoelace begins to fray—to unravel. During each cell division, part of the telomere is lost. Within approximately 120 years, the chromosome unravels, making cell replication impossible. Then the body can no longer repair itself and death is not far behind.

If you watch the news and the obituary column, you will find very few people who live to be over 120, or who have claimed to live more than 120 years. The book of Genesis is thought to have been written at least 1,300 years before Christ, or nearly 3,300 years ago. How could someone compile a worldwide human lifespan database three thousand years ago to suggest a maximum human lifespan? In other words, if there is not a God, who gave this information to the writer of Genesis? How could a near maximum 120 life span have been known so long ago?

It might be great if we could all live for nine hundred years, but what would the population be? A trillion? What kind of world would it be? How long would the line to the bathroom be? God thank You for shortening the human life span! Genesis 6:3 seems to describe a maximum or near-maximum life span, not a typical life span.

Another passage to consider. "And God said to Abram, "Know for certain that your descendants will be strangers in a land that is not theirs, where they will be enslaved and oppressed four hundred years. 14 "But I will also judge the nation whom they will serve; and afterward they will come out with many possessions. 15 "And as for you, you shall go to your fathers in peace; you shall be buried at a good old age. 16 "Then **in** the fourth generation they shall return here, for the iniquity of the Amorite is not yet complete." Genesis 15:13-16 (NASB). Genesis 15:16 mentions the "fourth generation," which might lead us to believe that dividing the four hundred years of enslavement by four would give us the life span of a generation. This would mean the span of a generation was one hundred years. Is the "fourth generation" in Genesis 15:16 directly related to the four hundred years in Genesis 15:13? It would require great Biblical knowledge to be certain. The passage may teach that a generation was one hundred years at that time. It might tell us that a generation is one hundred years. However, how many people live to one hundred? The passage does not seem to clearly state that a generation is one hundred years. The passage mentions that Abram's descendants will be enslaved for four hundred years and they would return to that place in the fourth generation. However it does not state that they would return in exactly 400 years at the very end of a fourth generation. If a generation were 90 years they could return in less than four hundred years and be in the fourth generation. It is unlikely that this passage describes a generation as 100 years.

If we add one hundred years to 1948, the things Jesus mentioned, which we will get to, would have until 2048 to occur. Considering the rate at which innovations have been occurring, self-aware computers or self-aware androids, quantum computers or atomic printers might become part of our individual lives. This would mean we would have entered into a new age, which Daniel 12:4 did not mention. Which would seem to imply the prophecy was wrong, when so many prophecies such as the birth of Israel in one day, have been fulfilled. This makes it unlikely that the generations Jesus mentions, has a life span of one hundred years.

There is another possibility. "As for the days of our life, they contain seventy years, or if due to strength, eighty years, …" (Ps. 90:10, NASB). Seventy or eighty years does seem to describe a typical human life span. We should be looking for a life span that Jesus would refer to, and Jesus frequently made reference to passages from the Old Testament. If seventy or eighty years defines a life span, it would not be possible to state a day or an hour. Yet it would allow us to know a general time period. A generation of seventy or eighty years is likely what we are looking for.

Jesus - "Truly I say to you, **this generation <u>will not pass away</u>, until all these things take place.**" (NASB, EM). He specifies "this generation." Which generation? The generation of people born at the time Israel was born (May 1948) would not pass away (die off) "until all these things take place"—all of the things Jesus talked about in Matthew 24.

I agree with Hal Lindsay's insight of using a generation to calculate when "these things could take place." [3]Adding 70 to 1948 gives us approximately 2018. Add 80 to 1948, and we get approximately 2028. With this information, we seem to have the answer to the disciples' question, "When will these things be?" (NASB). "The last days" likely start from approximately 1914, the beginning of the first age Daniel mentioned during the "end of time," a time period. We will see the things Jesus mentioned apparently started during the age that Daniel mentioned.

The time period then continues during the information age. Jesus also mentions the rebirth of Israel (which occurred in one day), a very unlikely event and perfect as evidence of fulfilled prophecy. From Israel's rebirth, which occurred within the time period Daniel mentions, Jesus mentions this generation taking the time line to the very end of the age.

If the "things" Jesus spoke of do not fall within this time frame, then either our understanding of the time or of the generation are wrong, or our understanding of the "things" themselves are wrong.

Please note the context Jesus spoke of: "Now learn the parable from the fig tree: when its branch has already become tender, and puts forth its leaves, you **know** that <u>**summer**</u> is near; 33 even so you too, <u>when you see all these things,</u> **recognize** that He is near, <u>right at the door.</u> 34 "Truly I say to you, this generation will not pass away until all these things take place." Matthew 24:32-34 (NASB, EM). Having given specific information about "when," Jesus then says, "**But** of the **day and hour no one knows** ..." Matthew 24:36 (NASB, EM). Jesus gives a season, "summer," a narrow time frame to "know." But this is not information that specifies the day or hour. In Jesus's spoken context, it is impossible to "know" or to "recognize" events if we can't "know," at least in general, the time period.

If we were to find two chapters in the Bible that say almost identical things, yet note a few details that are different, this could clear up questions and give new insights. This is very important in understanding the timing of the Great Tribulation and the rapture. Please read the following chapter, Revelation 6, which talks about the five seals, and think about what the imagery means.

6   Preparation: Know the Material, the Five Seals

"And I saw when the Lamb broke one of the seven seals, and I heard one of the four living creatures saying as with a voice of thunder, "Come." 2 And I looked, and behold, a white horse, and he who sat on it had a bow; and a crown was given to him; and he went out conquering, and to conquer. 3 And when He broke the second seal, I heard the second living creature saying, "Come." 4 And another, a red horse, went out; and to him who sat on it, it was granted to take peace from the earth, and that *men* should slay one another; and a great sword was given to him. 5 And when He broke the third seal, I heard the third living creature saying, "Come." And I looked, and behold, a black horse; and he who sat on it had a pair of scales in his hand. 6 And I heard as it were a voice in the center of the four living creatures saying, "A quart of wheat for a denarius, and three quarts of barley for a denarius; and do not harm the oil and the wine." 7 And when He broke the fourth seal, I heard the voice of the fourth living creature saying, "Come." 8 And I looked, and behold, an ashen horse; and he who sat on it had the name Death; and Hades was following with him. And authority was given to them over a fourth of the earth, to kill with sword and with famine and with pestilence and by the wild beasts of the earth. 9 And when He broke the fifth seal, I saw underneath the altar the souls of those who had been slain because of the word of God, and because of the testimony which they had maintained; 10 and they cried out with a loud voice, saying, "How long, O Lord, holy and true, wilt Thou refrain from judging and avenging our blood on those who dwell on the earth?" 11 And there was given to each of them a white robe; and they were told that they should rest for a little while longer, until *the number of* their fellow servants and their brethren who were to be killed even as they had been, should be completed also." (Rev. 6:1–11, NASB).

I encourage you think about what you have just read and ask yourself: What are these eleven verses of Revelation 6 talking about? You may want to write your thoughts down.

7   The Five Seals Relate to Matthew 24

Chapter 6 of the book of Revelation is in part written in imagery representing certain events. If you have not yet seen what God did in Revelation 6, I think you will be thrilled.

After reading the Bible for years, it came to mind that the first three horses of Revelation 6—the white horse, the red horse, and the black horse—sound very similar to some verses in Matthew 24. Revelation 6 continued to draw me in. Is there more to this than a similarity?

If the first three horses of Revelation 6 are the same three topics in a row as in Matthew 24, it is like a three-number combination lock on a gym locker. There are so many possible topics that finding the same three in the same order as a random coincidence is unlikely. If there are the same three topics in a row in Revelation 6 and Matthew 24, it seems intentional, and it seems there would be more insight to be found. Yet the question remained. Finally the answer came.

It may be easier to understand this concept if you purchase some colored pencils or colored pens and use them to underline words or phrases that convey the same subject. For example, use yellow to underline references to the "white horse", "I am the Christ," and "in my name" and so on. Highlighting similar ideas can help visualize the relationship between Revelation 6 and Matthew 24.

The White Horse

"And I looked, and behold, a **white horse**, and he who sat on it had a **bow**; and a **crown was given to him**; and he went out **conquering, and to conquer**." (Rev. 6:2, NASB, EM).

> "And Jesus answered and said to them, "See to it that no one misleads you. 5 "For **many will come in My name,**

saying, '**I am the Christ**', and will mislead many." (Matt. 24:4–5, NASB, EM).

White seems to represent the holiness of God. The crown seems to represent divinity—God. The crown was given to the one who sat on the horse. Since the crown was given to him, it is almost certain that it is not his. God created everything; everything is His. Therefore, there is nothing to be given to Christ, aside from praise, since He came as God in the flesh.

The crown may not even be real, but deceitful. "And through his shrewdness he will cause deceit to succeed by his influence; ..." (Daniel 8:25, NASB). Deceit and lies are the hallmark of false Christs and false Christianity. If the white horse represents false Christs, then the white horse should appear similar to Christ, since false Christs masquerade as Christ. We can be almost positive the passage is not speaking of Jesus but of false Christs.

As in spotting counterfeit money, we need to know exactly who the real Jesus is to recognize a counterfeit—a false Christ. Jesus and God the Father describe themselves in several biblical passages:

"... He who has seen Me has seen the Father; ..." (John 14:9, NASB)

"... for unless you believe that I am *He*, you will die in you sins." (John 8:24, NASB) The word "*He*" is added in the text.

"... before Abraham was born, I am." (John 8:58, NASB).

"And God said to Moses, "I AM WHO I AM;" and He said, "Thus you shall say to the sons of Israel, 'I AM has sent me to you.'" 15 ... This is My name forever, and this is My memorial-name to all generations." (Exod. 3:14–15, NASB).

We can see from these passages that Christ claims the same title of the Great I AM. Jesus is the Lord God Almighty in the flesh.

"...I am coming and I will dwell in your midst," declares the Lord." (Zech. 2:10, NASB)

"...AND THEY SHALL CALL HIS NAME IMMANUEL," which translated means, "GOD WITH US." (Matt. 1:23)

"...He has a name written, "KING OF KINGS, AND LORD OF LORDS." (Rev. 19:16, NASB).

The horse and rider referenced in the quotation from Revelation 19 are almost certainly not the same as the horse and rider in Revelation 6. There are clear differences between the two. There is no mention in Revelation 6 that the rider is called the "KING OF KINGS, AND LORD OF LORDS" (NASB), as in Revelation 19, nor is there any similar title given to the rider, implying deity, in Revelation 6.

Since Christ is God in the flesh, there is nothing to be given to Him aside from praise and obedience; all is His. The horse upon which the rider travels in Revelation 6:2 is white—white representing holiness. Yet the rider of the white horse carries a bow, which must represent eternal death—hell, which is the Antichrist's will. God draws people to Himself; He does not seem to force anyone to accept Him. In contrast, the rider of the white horse sets out "conquering, and to conquer." The Bible clearly states that God will pour out wrath, but this is not to conquer. It is not to force obedience. It is a consequence.

The rider is deceitful and lures people away from Christ to hell. The rider of the white horse likely represents false Christs who come in Jesus's name. This may include false Christianity. To be clear, the white horse almost definitely represents exactly what Christ was speaking of in Matthew 24:4-5: false Christs. Both passages seem to be saying exactly the same thing.

There is another point of evidence that helps to prove that the white horse in Revelation 6:2 represents false Christs and does not represent Christ. "And I saw heaven opened; and behold, a white horse, and He who sat upon it is called Faithful and True; and in righteousness He judges and makes war." (Rev. 19:11, NASB). The rider of the white horse in Revelation 6:2 is not called Faithful and True. More evidence latter.

If the following horses and seals continue to have the same topics as the verses in Matthew 24, it will give us further confidence that the white horse is false Christs.

The Red Horse

"And another, a **red** horse**,** went out; and to him who sat on it, it was **granted** to **take peace from the earth,** and that **men should slay** one another**;** and a **great sword** was **given** him**." (Rev. 6:4, NASB, EM)** "And you will be hearing of **wars** and rumors of wars; see that you are not frightened, for *those things* must take place, but that is not yet the end." (Matt. 24:6, NASB, EM)

The passage from Revelation mentions "take peace"; there was peace, and now that peace is taken away, which means war. "Men slay one another" is, of course, to kill others. A "great sword" is mentioned, a sword being a weapon normally used in combat - war. Just as false Christs may include false teaching – false doctrine, war as mentioned in Rev. 6 may also include fighting or murder by many, committed for the same reasons, such as hatred over opposing political or religious views and murder committed by people trying to survive. Choosing to kill because we don't like some one's religious view or political view or killing to satisfy need, is not Biblically justified. Although these deaths are not due to the nation's military forces, these specific deaths mentioned here are occurring due to the same convictions, desires or need on a large scale and therefore might be included as war. The horse's color, red, likely speaks of the blood of war. The red horse almost certainly represents exactly what Jesus spoke of in Matthew 24:6: war.

If this is true, there are now two verses back-to-back in Matthew 24 and Revelation 6 that speak of the same topics.

The Black Horse

"And when He broke the third seal, I heard the third living creature saying, "Come." And I looked, and behold, a **black horse**; and he who sat on it had a pair of scales in his hand. 6 And I heard as it were a voice in the center of the four living creatures saying, "**A quart of wheat for a denarius, and three quarts of barley for a denarius**; and do not harm the oil and the wine." (Rev. 6:5–6, NASB, EM)

"For nation will rise against nation, and kingdom against kingdom, and in various places there will be **famines** and earthquakes." (Matt. 24:7, NASB, EM)

A denarius was equal to a typical day's pay in that time, which means that these people work all day to buy one quart of wheat to feed themselves, no more. This is hardly enough to sustain the worker. For breadwinners who normally feed a wife, children, and perhaps parents, this is not nearly enough. Even three quarts of barley would not be enough.

We can have great confidence that the black horse of Revelation 6 is famine, just as Matthew 24:7 mentions famine. Thus, it seems clear that the first three horses in Revelation 6 and the false Christs, wars, and famines in Matthew 24 refer to the same things in the same order.

There are a few verses that may help confirm the meaning of the black horse. "The tongue of the infant cleaves to the roof of its mouth because of thirst; The little ones ask for bread, *But* no one breaks *it* for them." (Lam. 4:4, NASB). "**Their appearance is blacker than soot**, they are not recognized in the streets; Their skin is shriveled on their bones, it is withered, it has become like wood." (Lam. 4:8, NASB, EM). If these people naturally had a black skin tone, in the context of the passage, there would likely have been some clarification about their skin being blacker than soot. Instead, their black skin seems to be the result of famine. This horse's black color appears to confirm that black represents death by famine. If you except this explanation there are not three topics in the same order in Revelation six and Matthew 24.

The mention of kingdom against kingdom in Matthew 24:7 is almost certainly the conclusion of the subject of war in Matthew 24:6; not a new topic. In Matthew 24:7 Jesus mentions earthquakes. Some may therefore feel that this is another topic and therefore a break from all topics being the same and in the same order. There is another way to view it. Since

Jesus says "*and* earthquakes," He may have intended it to read: there will be famines which by the way, will be accompanied by earthquakes. Understandably, this may not be satisfying.

The Ashen Horse

Please be patient, as the ashen horse is the most difficult to understand. Once the ashen horse is understood, the rest of Revelation 6 is easier to understand. You may be hesitant to accept the suggested meaning of the ashen horse. Yet if the suggested meaning is correct or nearly correct, everything else comes together.

"And I looked, and behold, an **ashen horse**; and he who sat on it had the name Death; and Hades was following with him. And authority was given to them **over a fourth of the earth**, to **kill with sword and with famine** and with pestilence and by the wild beasts of the earth." (Rev. 6:8, NASB, EM). What does this mean?

The rider of the ashen horse has a sword the same power as the red horse—war. The ashen horse also has the power of the black horse—famine. These powers appear in the same order as the red horse and the black horse. However, the passage does not appear to speak of a white horse, which of course came before the red and the black horses. Nor does there seem to be any mention of false Christs, at least not that is obvious. The three horses came in the same order as the false Christs, wars, and famine.

The plagues of the ashen horse "kill with the sword," and "famine" are in the same order as the red horse and the black horse. Is the white horse of Revelation 6:2 to be found in Revelation 6:8, before war and famine? Since Revelation 6 speaks by means of symbolism, the white horse may be mentioned symbolically. Is there any symbolic representation of false Christs?

"And I looked, and behold, an **ashen horse**; and he who sat on it had the name **Death**; and **Hades** was following with him..."(Rev.6:8, NASB, EM).

Notice that Hades, which is hell, is following death. Hades has no power over those who have accepted Christ. False Christs and false religion act to separate people from Christ, leading to hell those who do not accept Christ. Therefore Death and Hades likely represent false Christs, since they preach a false gospel that does not lead to faith in Christ. Converts to false Christianity and those who deny Christ die without Christ, which leads to spiritual death, physical death, and then hell—Hades. In Genesis Satan's temptation of Adam and Eve results in separation from God and eternal life is lost - death. Satan is the one who planed and implemented death. It is appropriate that Satan would be called – named Death.

This imagery seems a bit vague. There is no specific mention of Jesus, as in Matthew 24:5, "I am the Christ" (NASB). Yet there is no statement, no information in Revelation 6:8 that would lead us to say that Death and Hades do *not* represent false Christs.

It is also possible that Death and Hades are intended as a broader comment that includes false Christianity. Though it may seem a stretch, Death and Hades almost certainly represent the white horse, as Death and Hades appear in the same place in the order—the white horse, the red horse, and the black horse. The description of the ashen horse does not mention white or a crown but uses a different imagery to describe the same idea. The imagery of Death and Hades focuses on the result of the deception of false Christs, which is in harmony with the outcome of those who, in Matthew 24:4, "mislead many" (NASB) delivering to hell. They are almost certainly the same.

The color of this horse in the NASB version is ashen. Other Bible versions translated the description as "pale" or "dappled" or even "pale green." So which is it?

Green does not seem to be the intent of the text. The only manner in which green might seem to fit would be if it were intended to describe a feeling of sickness from suffering. Yet green does not seem to fit the context. The word *ashen* has a suffix, -en, which means "like" or "similar to"—like ashes. The root word, *ash*, is of course what is left over after wood or other flammable materials burn. The color name means "like the color of ashes."

Ashen and *dappled* are essentially the same. Ashes are in general gray. Among ashes one often finds other colors like white, black, gray ashes, and even colors from various elements, including red. Ashes are actually a mix of colors. The color of the ashen horse seems to be a mix of the white, black, and red horses. The ashen horse seems to represent all three previous horses, with the added powers of pestilence, wild beasts, and authority to kill over a fourth of the earth. This is an increase, an ability to harm that is even worse than the three previous horses combined.

This seems to be the primary point of the ashen horse. Wars occur more often and are more destructive. Famine kills more people. False Christs and/or charlatans claiming to represent Christianity deliver more to hell. The additional suffering from pestilence and wild beasts, which may feast on the weak or dead, explains that life is getting worse.

Is there a verse in Matthew 24 that comes soon after the references to false Christs, war, and famine, and means the same thing as the ashen horse? "But all these things are *merely* the **beginning of birth pangs.**" (Matt. 24:8, NASB, EM).

Generally, I have heard, when a woman has her second birth pang, or contraction, it is likely to be stronger than the first. The time between the second and third contractions is generally shorter than the time between the first and the second. The birth pangs keep getting stronger, more severe, as the time between them becomes shorter. In the same way, this verse tells us that wars become worse and occur more frequently. The same is then true for pestilence, false Christs, famines, and earthquakes.

In Matthew 24:8, Christ is saying that false Christs, war, and famine are merely the beginning of suffering. These things will continue to get worse, leading to "the end," the Great Tribulation, which has not yet come. The ashen horse of Revelation 6:8 almost definitely represents the birth pangs in Matthew 24:8. Suffering continues to get worse.

The references to Death and Hades may give further insight into the white horse, perhaps implying false doctrine—false teaching, maybe. Although a bit obscure, the ashen horse seems to fit birth pangs to a *T*. The ashen horse is the fourth parallel between Matthew 24 and Revelation 6, and in consecutive order.

The more parallels there are, the more unlikely it is that these have occurred by chance. Does the parallel continue?

Contemporary Martyrs

"And when He broke the fifth seal, I saw underneath the **altar** the **souls of those who had been slain because of the word of God**, and because of the **testimony** which they had maintained; 10 and they cried out with a loud voice, saying, "How long, O Lord, holy and true, wilt Thou refrain from judging and avenging our **blood** on those who dwell on the earth?" 11 And there was given to each of them a **white robe**; and they were told that they should rest for a little while longer, until *the number* of their **fellow servants** and **their brethren** who were **to be killed** even as they had been, **should be completed** also." (Rev. 6:9-11, NASB, EM)

After describing the birth pangs, Christ continues. "Then they will deliver **you to tribulation**, and will **kill you, and you will be hated by all nations on account of My name**." (Matt. 24:9, NASB, EM).

It is important to understand that the word "tribulation" by itself simply means suffering. Used by itself "tribulation" does not mean the "Great Tribulation," or "the Great Suffering." Capitalizing and quotation marks are being used with the phrase "Great Tribulation" to make a distinction between general suffering (tribulation) from the specific time of great suffering, the "Great Tribulation."

"These things I have spoken to you, that in Me you may have peace. **In the world you have tribulation,** but take courage; I have overcome the world." (John 16:33, NASB, EM). In this passage, Jesus explains that if you live in this world, you will experience some suffering, some tribulation. Every individual will have his or her own suffering and to varying degrees. Again, this is not a reference to the extreme suffering of the "Great Tribulation"— the greatest suffering the world has ever known.

When Jesus says, "Then they will deliver you to tribulation, and *will kill you, and you will be hated by all nations on account of My* name." (Matt. 24:9, NASB, EM), Jesus is saying that some of you will suffer and some or many of you will suffer and be killed for belief in Christ. However, this is not the "Great Tribulation."

When Jesus says, "They will deliver you to tribulation, and kill you" (NASB), He also tells us why: "on account of My name." Clearly these people who believe in Jesus, have committed their lives to Him, and are being martyred—killed for believing in Christ. This seems be the same line of thought as in Matthew 10:32–33 "Everyone therefore who shall confess Me before men, I will also confess him before My Father who is in heaven. 33 "But whoever shall deny Me before men, I will also deny him before My Father who is in heaven." (NASB).

Most of us in the United States have not literally seen people killed for their faith in Christ. For that reason, many have thought the end must not be that close. In the United States neither we nor our friends have been forcibly taken to trial for our faith and killed. True, we have seen attacks on freedom of speech, but no executions here. We have been very fortunate, unlike believers living in China, North Korea, and some Muslim nations.

In fact, there have been more Christians martyred for their faith in the last one hundred years than in all previous history. If you research this, you can find sources stating that 50–65 percent of all Christians martyred in all history have been killed in the past hundred years.[1]

We in the United States have been very fortunate. This may change in the coming ten to twelve years as history unfolds, conforming to Scripture. Confession of faith in Jesus Christ and the short suffering of death are a small price to pay for an eternity in heaven with the Lord.

"And when He broke the fifth seal, I saw **underneath the altar** the **souls** of those who had **been slain because of the word of God**, and **because of the testimony which they had maintained**; 10 and they cried out with a loud voice, saying, "How long, O Lord, holy and true, wilt Thou refrain from judging and **avenging our blood** on those who dwell on the earth?" 11 And there was given to each of them a white robe; and they were told that they should rest for a little while longer, until *the number of* their **fellow servants** and their **brethren who were to be killed** even **as they had been**, should be completed also." (Rev. 6:9–11, NASB, EM).

Revelation 6:9 mentions "those slain" because of their "testimony" to "the word of God." This is obviously talking about Christians killed for their faith as in Matthew 24:9. The passage continues talking about their fellow "servants," "brethren," fellow brothers in Christ who are to "be killed," martyred also. These Christians under the altar in heaven are waiting until the last Christians are martyred, so that vengeance from God will be poured out on those who martyred them. As in Matthew 24:9, Revelation 6:9–11 is also talking about followers of Christ who are to be killed, martyred.

With the four horses, and now Christians being martyred for their faith under the fifth seal, we have five topics in consecutive order in which Matthew 24 and Revelation 6 deliver the same message. If this is the case, Revelation may continue in chronological order with Matthew. If it does, this may help us better understand what will happen at the time of the end.

The imagery of the sixth chapter of Revelation might lead us to conclude that it describes the beginning of the "Great Tribulation". But does it? Some Bibles have a heading above Revelation 6 that says something like "the four horses of the apocalypse." This also could make us think the chapter is about the "Great Tribulation."

The primary meaning of *apocalypse* is "to reveal": revelation. Things are being revealed. *Apocalypse* can also mean the last book of the Bible, the book of Revelation. Those who have not looked up the definition may have in mind the language of chapter 6, which brings to mind horrific depictions.

Given movies like *Apocalypse Now* and phrases like "the zombie apocalypse," these terrifying images could lead some to believe that *apocalypse* means the same event as the "Great Tribulation". But *apocalypse* means to reveal, and *tribulation* means to suffer. Apocalypse and the "Great Tribulation" are not the same.

Is there anything to indicate that the Great Tribulation has begun within the first five seals? It should all become clear. These statements do not mean that the "Great Tribulation" will not be worse than what many think of when thinking of the Apocalypse. The horses in the book of Revelation truly are giving revelation of what is to come.

The following chapter, "The First Parallel View," is arranged in columns. These columns are not *intended to be read in the usual way: that is, all of the left-hand column and then all of the right-hand column.* All emphasis in is mine, possibly aside from some italic.

Instead of reading the left column first and then the right column, please read a few of verses in the left-hand column and then a few verses in the right column. Then notice the common topic in bold print in both passages. Continue to the end in the same manner. The topics from Revelation 6 and Matthew 24 are the same and in the same order. The intention is to allow us to visualize what has been discussed.

8   The First Parallel View

Revelation 6:1 "And I saw when the Lamb broke one of the seven seals, and I heard one of the four living creatures saying as with a voice of thunder, "Come." 2 And I looked, and behold, a **white horse**, and he who sat on it had a **bow**; and a **crown** was given to him; and he went out **conquering**, and to **conquer.** 3 And when He broke the second seal, I heard the second living creature saying, "Come." 4 And another, a **red horse**, went out; and to him who sat on it, it was granted to **take peace from the earth**, and that *men* **should slay one another**; and a **great sword** was given to him. 5 And when He broke the third seal, I heard the third living creature saying, "Come." And I looked, and behold, a **black horse**; and he who sat on it had a **pair of scales** in his hand. 6 And I heard as it were a voice in the center of the four living creatures saying, "**A quart of wheat for a denarius, and three quarts of barley for a denarius;** and do not harm the oil and the wine." (NASB, EM).

Matthew 24:3 "…Tell us, when will these things be, and what will be the sign of Your coming, and of the end of the age?" 4 And Jesus answered and said to them, "See to it that no one misleads you. 5 "For many will **come in My name, saying, 'I am the Christ,'** and will **mislead** many." (NASB, EM).

[The white horse is false Christs in Matt.24:5. The red horse, a great sword & "slay men" are wars in Matthew 24:6.]

Matthew 24:6 "And you will be hearing of **wars and rumors of wars**; see that you are not frightened, for *those things* must take place, but that is not yet the end. 7 "For nation will rise against nation, and **kingdom against kingdom**, and in various places there will be **famines** and earthquakes." (NASB, EM).

[The black horse & quart of wheat for a full days wage (a denarius) Is famine in Matt 24:7.]

[Verse numbers have been maintained for easy reference].

Revelation 6:7 "And when He broke the fourth seal, I heard the voice of the fourth living creature saying, "Come." 8 And I looked, and behold, an **ashen horse**; and he who sat on it had the name **Death**; and **Hades was following** with him. And authority was given to them over a **fourth of the earth**, to **kill with sword** and with **famine** and with **pestilence** and by the **wild beasts** of the earth." (NASB, EM).

Revelation 6:9 "And when He broke the fifth seal, I saw underneath the **altar** the souls of those who had been slain because of the word of God, and because of the testimony which they had maintained; 10 and they cried out with a loud voice, saying, "How long, O Lord, holy and true, wilt Thou refrain from judging and avenging our blood on those who dwell on the earth?" 11 And there was given to each of them a **white robe**; and they were told that they should rest for a little while longer, until *the number of* **their fellow servants** and **their brethren who were to be killed** even as they had been, should be complete also." (NASB, EM).

[In Rev. 6:8 "Death" and "Hades" represent false Christs (Rev. 6:2) who lead people away from Christ. When they Die (Death) they then go to Hell (Hades). "Kill with the sword" is the Red horse—war. Rev. 6:4 Famine is the Black horse. Rev.6:5 & Pestilence & wild beasts: things get worse.] Matt. 24:8 "But all **these things** are merely the beginning of **birth pangs**." (NASB, EM).

[Birth pangs get worse. Rev. 6:7 & 8 & Matt. 24:8 are the same. Things get worse. White robes indicate the martyred are Christians. The altar is in a holy place (heaven). Rev. 4:1 is in heaven. Rev. 6:11: they should rest—wait a little while longer. "Fellow servants" are Christians alive on earth as are "their brethren," who are to be martyred—killed for their belief in Christ and their witness.] Matt. 24:9 "Then they will deliver you to tribulation, and will **kill you**, and you will be hated by all nations on **account of My name**." (NASB, EM).

[Rev. 6:11 and Matt. 24:9 state the same topics in the same order.]

9   Putting the Puzzle Together: The First Five Seals

In Matthew 24:3, Jesus's disciples ask, "...when will these things be?" "and what will be the sign of Your coming, and the end of the age?" (NASB). Jesus then refers to the writings of Daniel in Matthew 24:15, in relation to prophecy of the last days. Jesus refers to Daniel since he is describes the same overall time period that Daniel does and adds other details.

Have the things Jesus spoke of been occurring during the time period spoken of, which seems start about 1914 and end by approximately 2028?

War

There have been many wars throughout history, even in the period since the 1500s. It would be overwhelming to consider them all here. There are a few things that should be clear, though, without a lengthy consideration of history. Approximately fifty nations were involved in World War I, approximately 113 nations involved in World War II.[1] Some nations were separated by large distances and used weapons greatly advanced from previous wars.

In the 1800s, rifles, some metallic cartridges, the hand-cranked Gatling gun, sailing ships, and some steam ships were used in war. World War I brought the Maxim machine gun, the first automatic machine gun (nicknamed the devil's paint brush), the first combustion-engine-powered tanks, mustard gas, steel diesel ships, and triplanes. As the birth pangs grew, World War II brought larger ships with huge guns, formidable tanks, aluminum B-52s, and the atomic bomb.

With such horrific wars being waged by such ruthless leaders as Hitler, it is no wonder that many, especially those living in war zones, thought they might be living in the Great Tribulation. From the countries that were involved in fighting during World War I, More than 28 million people were killed, wounded, or missing in action during World War I.

World War II involved approximately 100 million military troops, with an estimated 50–80 million killed, the red horse.

Daniel mentioned a time during the latter Industrial Age, and Jesus mentioned war, an increase in war – the ashen horse and the generation that saw Israel born. World War I and World War II occurred during the Industrial Age. People were rushing across the earth during these wars. The people who thought they might be living during the Great Tribulation were not. However, they were almost certainly living during the last days, as indicated by Daniel.

After World War II came the Korean War, the Vietnam War, the wars in Iraq and Afghanistan, and numerous other wars, including tribal wars. As the birth pangs continue, we now have stealth fighter jets, smart bombs, GPS coordinates, and nuclear Inter Continental Ballistic Missiles. All of this echoes Jesus's statement, if not also confirms His prophetic words about the red horse of war. The escalation seems to also confirm the birth pangs: the ashen horse. These things will get worse. The data on World War l and World War ll come from Wikipedia.com.

Famine

Four unthinkable famines occurred in China over nearly a half century, from 1810 through 1849, taking the lives of an estimated 45 million people. There were other famines in the 1800s, and though these resulted in enormous loss of life, famines in the 1900s caused even more loss of life. You may want to go to Wikipedia.com to find this and even more data about famines. (https./en.wikipedia.org/wiki/List_of_famines) 3/3/2016 Death tolls are approximate. Data gleaned from Wikipedia.

From 800 through 884, there were three famines that we know of. They occurred in Mayan areas, with deaths estimated in the millions.

From 927 through 928, one famine is noted, with no data available regarding deaths.

From 1005 through 1097, there were six known famines, with approximately 100,000 deaths in France alone.

From 1230 through 1299, there were five known famines, with approximately 20,000 deaths in London alone.

From 1315 through 1387, there were four known famines, with no data available regarding the death toll.

From 1396 through 1461, there were four known famines, with no data available regarding the death toll.

From 1504 through 1586, there were six known famines, with no data available regarding the death toll.

From 1601 through 1697, there were fifteen known famines, with roughly 6.8 million related deaths.

From 1702 through 1792, there were twenty-two known famines, with roughly 34.2 million related deaths.

From 1810 through 1902, there were twenty-four known famines, with roughly 53 million related deaths.

The following data on famines falls within the time frame indicated by Daniel and Jesus:

From 1914 through 1936, there were fourteen known famines, with roughly 23 million related deaths.

From 1914 through 2000, there were thirty-nine known famines, with roughly 55 million related deaths.

From 1998 through 2012, there were four known famines, with roughly 1 million related deaths.

This is a total of roughly 79 million deaths in approximately 98ninety-eight years that fall within the time period mentioned by Jesus and Daniel.

Estimates suggest that the percentage of large fish in the sea has fallen significantly and is still falling. This leaves less fish from the oceans to feed a growing world population (https://en.wikipedia.org/wik./Coral_bleaching;) 3/28/2016 www.huffingtonpost.com/2011/02/coral-reefs-may-be/gone-b_n_827709.hdtml ; 3/28/2016 news.nationalgeographic.com/news/2003/05/0515_030515_fishdecline.html). 3/28/2016

As with the fish population a significant percentage of the oceans' coral has died. This is alarming since the coral reefs are fish habitats, and further alarming since they absorb CO_2, therefore reducing greenhouse gas.[1]

Clearly, it is a bit difficult to compare the number of famines and the number of deaths the further back in history we go. It is important to have reasonably accurate data, so that we can make a reasonably informed decision. We do have data that people have diligently researched to obtain. We can use this information to make our own decisions.

Have the famines Christ spoke of been occurring and gradually increasing? Have wars, starting with World War I, been escalating? Do the famines and wars that have been occurring fulfill the prophecies of the red horse, the black horse, and the ashen horse?

What has been occurring during the time period referred to by Daniel and Jesus when they spoke of the end of the age and Christ's return?

The Five Seals Visual

The Industrial Age			The Information Age		
World War I	World War II	Korean War	Vietnam, Iraq, Afghanistan		
1900 1914	1940 1948 Israel reborn		2000	2021	2028

More people martyred for their faith than in all past history

1959–61 Chinese Famine: 15–40 million die. 1996 North Korean famine: 3.5 million die

Earthquakes in Alaska, California, Mexico City, Haiti, and Japan; the Philippine tsunami

Pestilence: the flu strains, Ebola, malaria, etc.

Earthquakes

On January 23, 1556, an earthquake took an estimated 830,000 lives, the greatest estimated death toll in history from an earthquake. This earthquake's intensity has been estimated to be 8.3 on the Richter scale. (The earthquake occurred before there was a Richter scale or the instrument Richter invented to measure the severity of earthquakes). Death tolls are approximate.

For the century 1600 through 1700, there were twelve recorded earthquakes, estimated to have been from 6.8 to 9 on the Richter scale, with roughly 168,000 related deaths.

For the century 1700 through 1800, there were twenty-five recorded earthquakes, estimated to have been from 5.9 to 9 on the Richter scale, with roughly 584,000 related deaths.

For the century 1800 through 1900, there were approximately fifty-one recorded earthquakes, estimated to have been from 6.3 to 9 on the Richter scale, with roughly 126,000 related deaths.

From 1901 through 1910, approximately 18eighteen earthquakes were recorded, estimated to have been from 6 to 8.8 on the Richter scale, with roughly 127,000 related deaths.

The following earthquake data represents events that occurred during the approximate time Daniel and Jesus spoke of as the last days.

From 1911 through 1920, seventeen earthquakes were recorded, estimated to have been from 6.5 to 8.6 on the Richter scale, with roughly 286,000 related deaths.

From 1921 through 1930, twenty-five earthquakes were recorded, estimated to have been from 6.1 to 8.5 on the Richter scale, with roughly 193,000 related deaths.

From 1931 through 1940, thirty-four earthquakes were recorded, estimated to have been from 5.8 to 8.8 on the Richter scale, with roughly 92,000 related deaths.

From 1941 through 1950, thirty-two earthquakes were recorded, registering from 6.1 to 8.2 on the Richter scale, with roughly 41,000 related deaths.

From 1951 through 1960, thirty-one earthquakes were recorded, registering from 5.7 to 9.5 on the Richter scale, with roughly 17,000 related deaths.

From 1961 through 1970, thirty-nine earthquakes were recorded, registering from 5.9 to 9.2 on the Richter scale, with roughly 102,000 related deaths.

From 1971 through 1980, thirty-four earthquakes were recorded, registering from 6.1 to 8.2 on the Richter scale, with roughly 342,000 related deaths.

From 1981 through 1990, thirty-four earthquakes were recorded, registering from 5.5 to 8 on the Richter scale, with roughly 86,000 related deaths.

From 1991 through 2000, forty-five earthquakes were recorded, registering from 5.4 to 8.2 on the Richter scale, with roughly 40,000 related deaths.

From 2001 through 2010, 340 earthquakes were recorded, registering from 3.5 to 8.8 on the Richter scale, with roughly 608,000 related deaths.

From 2011 through 2014 (a shorter time period), 128 earthquakes were recorded, registering from 4.5 to 9.0 on the Richter scale, with roughly 19,000 deaths.

Summarizing this data: from 1911 through 2014, there were 714 recorded earthquakes resulting in approximately 1.8 million deaths. Earthquake data gleaned from Wikipedia.com. (https://en.wikipedia.org/wiki/Historical_earthquakes) 3/3/2016

Scientists can view an earthquake's damage and estimate the force exerted on specific structures. However, individual judgment may not stick to standard measures well. Richter's invention of the Richter scale created an objective standard that can be lost with individuals' varying perception. His scale was published in 1935. It may be difficult to know just how accurate the records are from the era before the Richter scale. We hopefully have the general concept we need.

Have earthquakes and their toll been increasing like birth pangs, as the ashen horse would indicate? Looking at the data from 1914 through 2014, there are two things in which we can have some confidence. The number of earthquakes per decade seems fairly consistent until roughly the year 2000. The death toll rises, yet not steadily, and then jumps and increases several-fold. There were thirty-four earthquakes from 1981 through 1990, then 340 earthquakes documented from 2001 through 2010.

Should we make light of the prophecy, thinking that the death toll should have risen also since the earth's population has risen? However, the prophecy only mentions earthquakes. It specifies that earthquakes will increase, with no mention of the death toll. Obviously more deaths likely occur due to greater population.

Someone might make the argument that there are periods of greater seismic activity and periods with less activity, and the current age is simply a period of relatively more seismic activity. Exactly correct—that is the point. The prophecy simply states that the period of time being spoken of will be a period of significant and increasing seismic activity.

Pestilence

Included under the category of pestilence are the major communicable diseases from each era, such as influenza, the Black Death, smallpox, Ebola, malaria, and so on. Death tolls are approximate. Data on pestilence gleaned from Wikipedia.com. (https://wikipedia.org/wiki/Historcial_earthquakes) 3/3/16

From 1600 through 1690, there were approximately twenty one outbreaks with roughly 500,000 associated deaths.

From 1702 through 1798, there were approximately thirty-two outbreaks with roughly 100,000 associated deaths.

From 1800 through 1906, there were approximately fifty-nine outbreaks with roughly 2.5 million associated deaths.

From 1899 through 1922, there were approximately nine outbreaks with roughly 75.8 million associated deaths.

From 1942 through 2000, there were approximately eighteen outbreaks with roughly 33.02 million associated deaths.

From 2001 through 2014, there were approximately fifty outbreaks with roughly 380,000 associated deaths.

The time frame Daniel mentions as the start of the last days seems to start about 1914, approximately two-thirds of the way through the 1899–1922 pestilence. Using a third of 75 million deaths from 1899–1922, plus deaths from 1914 thru 2014, would yield approximately 58 million deaths by pestilence from 1914 to 2014. The population increased from 1914 to 2014;

however, Christ did not say why pestilence would increase or how, just that it would become worse. Have deaths by pestilence been increasing? The approximate 58 million is mentioned for a comparison to other time periods. Pestilence, along with false Christs, may be the most difficult case to make for birth pangs.

False Christs

Many of us remember David Koresh, the leader of the Branch Dravidians, who claimed to be a messiah and led many of his followers to a fiery death. About three dozen people historically have made high-profile claims to be a Christian messiah or Jesus Christ Himself. (https.//en.wikipedia.org/wiki/List_of_messiah_claimants) 3/28/2016

There are many congregations that use "church" in their name and claim Christ in some way. Yet in many cases the teachings of these "churches" are contrary to what the Bible states. The teachings go against the fundamental Biblical principles stated in the Nicene Creed. Since these "churches" claim to speak for Christ, yet teach other doctrines, Christ may consider their leaders to have falsely come in His name.

A local rumor has it that a pastor in a not too distant community has claimed to have no sin. Only God is holy—that is, without sin. "If we say that we have no sin, we are deceiving ourselves, and the truth is not in us." (1 John 1:8, NASB). To say we have no sin is essentially to take on an attribute of God. Whether this specific rumor is true or not, if there are others making similar claims, they would likely also fit the category of "false Christs."

The Reverend Jeremiah Wright made a radical statement: "God damn America for treating our citizens as less than human. God damn America for as long as she acts like she is God and is supreme" (http://famousquotesandproverbs.blogspot.com/2008/03/quotes-made-famous-by-rev-jeremiah.html). 3/28/2016

Many people think of America as a land called America. However, America would not be called America without those who have lived here and named it America. For a great part, America is the people who live in and represent America.

"I SOLEMNLY charge you in the presence of God and of Christ Jesus, who is to judge the living and the dead, …" (2 Tim. 4:1, NASB). Only God our Creator has the authority to damn people to hell. In damning America to hell, the Reverend Wright has claimed an attribute of God, whether he realized it or not. Having claimed an attribute of God by damning, he has likely come in Christ's name.

"The Lord is not slow about His promise, as some count slowness, but is patient toward you, not wishing for any to perish but for all to come to repentance." (2 Pet. 3:9, NASB). God does not want anyone to be judged to hell.

Though the Reverend Wright asked for God to damn America for acting like God, Wright himself acted like God by damning and thereby did the very thing he condemned.

The implications of Reverend Wright's statement –"God damn America" have probably not been recognized even by a few in Reverend Wright's congregation. In damning America without any qualification, he is damning all Americans—you and I, himself, and even his own congregation. Wasn't Barack Obama among those in the Reverend Wright's congregation?

There are many who qualify as "false Christs" or those who come in His name, and their number seems to be increasing. If you ask Christians who remember the 1960s, you are likely to hear that false Christian teaching has been on the rise since then. Yes, there would then be a debate about the very definition of a Christian. We need pay close attention to the statements people make.

If the ashen horse includes those teaching false statements about Christ and Christianity, and further, if Christ's statement "mislead many" is taken to refer to false teaching, then it would not be a stretch to say there appear to be many falsely coming in Christ's name.

False Christs are one of the more difficult "things" to quantify. Are there, and have there been, many coming in Christ's name? We will see if there is a significant change in the not too distant future.

We who have been living through the latter part of the Industrial Age and into the Information Age have almost certainly been living during the time of the four horses, false Christs, wars, famines and the ashen horse. We have seen increases in these things. We have seen the birth pangs associated with the ashen horse and the fifth seal. All of these "things" we have seen might be said to be giving birth to the very "end of the age," the "Great Tribulation."

Birth pangs will lead to the greatest suffering in human history, the "Great Tribulation." This is like the final scene in a play or movie, in which the good guys and the bad guys duke it out, and Christ is the hero. In fact, Christ rides in on a white horse, just like the last scene in so many cowboy movies. "And I saw heaven opened; and behold, a white horse, and He who sat upon it is called Faithful and True; and in righteousness He judges and wages war." (Rev. 19:11, NASB).

Not by Chance

Observing the way in which the first three horses in Revelation 6 represent the same three topics in the same order as in Matthew 24, there is a comparison to be made. In gym class, you probably had a combination lock. If you didn't have a gym locker, you probably had a hall locker with a combination.

Most of these locks have about 30-40 numbers on them. Entering three numbers in the correct order unlocks the lock. It is very unlikely that someone could guess which numbers were in the combination and what order they needed to be entered in to unlock the lock. For this reason, the locks are considered a safe way to protect belongings.

In the same way, we can compare the topics of the first three horses of Revelation to three numbers on a combination lock. If these same three topics show up in the same order as the topics in Matthew 24, it is as if someone unlocked your school locker by chance—only less likely. Revelation 6 is difficult to understand; using Matthew 24 to understand Revelation 6 is similar to someone telling us the combination to their gym locker.

The Bible has many more topics than a typical lock has numbers: love, hate, greed, forgiveness, discipline—perhaps a hundred topics. This of course means the likelihood that the same three topics would show up in the same order is much more unlikely than unlocking a gym lock by chance.

When the topics of the fourth and fifth seal are added to this list, there is a sequence of five matching topics. By the time the parallel between Matthew 24 and Revelation 6 is complete, we will have seen nine topics in a row. The probability of this occurring by chance is unreasonable. Jesus was giving an explanation in Matthew 24, and Revelation 6 tells us that Jesus Christ is giving John revelation in the book of Revelation.

Unfortunately for John and the other apostles, they had no photocopiers, no Xerox machines. Though many handwritten copies of the apostles' letters were made, there were not enough for everyone. Therefore it may have been rare for John to see copies of the writings of other disciples. Although possible, it seems unlikely that John had a copy of the book of Matthew with him on the Isle of Patmos, to use in fabricating the book of Revelation. The disciples were committed to following Christ to the point of martyrdom. To fabricate Revelation 6 would have been unthinkable. Yet it is far too improbable for this lengthy and identical subject order to have happened by chance. How did it happen?

Jesus ordered the topics in Revelation 6 to be the same as in Matthew 24. Christ converted the explanation in Matthew 24 to apocalyptic imagery in Revelation 6, included a split verse in Revelation 6 to match the ones in Matthew 24 and Daniel 12. Without taking our focus off the nine topics, Christ slipped in another explanation in the five seals. Christ left it for the minds He gave us to find—or, more likely, He slipped the thought into our minds directly—that Matthew 24 and Revelation 6 spoke of the same things. Thank You, Lord.

10 Brethren in Christ: A Teaching Error

There is a false teaching that states that the Church—Christians—are not mentioned as being on earth after chapter 4 in the book of Revelation. This needs to be addressed now.

"And when He broke the fifth seal, I **saw underneath the altar the souls** of those who had been **slain because of the word of God**, and because of the **testimony which they had maintained; 10** and they cried out with a loud voice, saying, "How long, O Lord, holy and true, wilt Thou refrain from judging and avenging our blood on those who dwell on the earth?" 11 And there was given to each of them a white robe; and they were told that *they should rest for a little while longer*, **until** *the number of* their **fellow servants** and **their brethren** who were **to be killed** even as they had been, should be completed also." (Rev. 6:9–11, NASB, EM)

These souls cry out for vengeance, which God says is His to carry out. "… VENGEANCE IS MINE, I WILL REPAY," says the Lord." (Rom. 12:19, NASB). God then tells them, in Revelation 6:11, to wait in ease, as there are more Christians who will be martyred before His vengeance is carried out. Christian souls under the altar are waiting for their brethren, fellow Christians, to be martyred before vengeance is carried out. These Christians are yet to be killed so, Christians—the Church—are clearly alive on earth at this time, in fact now, in 2016 and until the rapture. Assuming we are in the time period that is being suggested, those Christians in Revelation 6:11 would include many of us. Why?

"Then they will deliver you to tribulation, and will kill you …" (Matt. 24:9, NASB). This is the subject found in Revelation 6:11 " …their fellow servants and their brethren to be killed …" (NASB). As previously shown, this is the fifth seal and is one of the "things" Jesus mentioned occurring "when": likely from 1914 as Jesus mentioned Daniel, and during the generation Jesus mentioned starting in 1948 and going through approximately 2028. Those of us who are Christians, living during that time period from 1914 - 1948 and on until the rapture, are almost certainly among those mentioned in Revelation 6:11.

At this point in Matthew 24:9, the rapture has not yet occurred, just as it has not yet occurred in Revelation 6:9-11. Also the Great Tribulation has not started. It is important to understand that Christians, we who are still on earth at this time, 2016 and until the rapture, are almost certainly living during the period spoken of in Revelation 6. This can be said with confidence but not certainly.

At this point some of you may be in a quandary. You may have been told by a pastor, elder, or preacher you saw on TV that the Church is not on earth after Revelation chapter 4. They made a mistake, just as this author will from time to time or more often.

"Immediately I was in the Spirit; and behold, a throne was standing in heaven, and One sitting on the throne. 3 And He who was sitting was like a jasper stone and a sardius in appearance; and *there was* a rainbow around the throne, like an emerald in appearance. 4 And around the throne were twenty-four thrones; and upon the thrones I *saw* twenty-four elders sitting, clothed in white garments, and golden crowns on their heads." (Rev. 4:2–4, NASB).

These are verses that have been used to say that the "entire Church" is in heaven at this point, and therefore the rapture has already occurred. The claim is, that since the elders have "white garments" and "crowns on their heads" and are "sitting on thrones" around God's throne, is somehow proof they have been raptured before the tribulation. At best that is a guess, and it is wrong.

Clearly there are twenty-four elders sitting on thrones, clothed in white garments, with golden crowns on their heads. However, where is the evidence, a statement of any kind in the book of Revelation that says they were caught up—raptured? No such statement is made. Unfortunately, this concept is somewhere between conjecture and a wild guess.

Our understanding of who these elders are, is very limited. Due to the way they are spoken of in the Bible, some could be Christ's twelve disciples (but not Judas) – "Then Peter answered and said to Him, "Behold, we have left everything and followed You; what then will there be for us?" 28 And Jesus said to them, "Truly I say to your, that you who have followed Me, in the regeneration when the Son of Man will sit on His glorious throne, you also shall sit upon twelve thrones, ..." (Matt:19:27,28, NASB)

Rev. 4:2 & 5:1&7 mention Christ the Lamb on His throne. It would seem that there is probably but not certainly only one throne room in heaven and therefore just these twenty-four thrones. If that is the case and twelve disciples occupy twelve of the thrones, there would not be enough thrones for twenty four people—elders, coming from a rapture. Nor does there seem to be any mention of a rapture in Rev. chapters 1–4. Those on the twenty-four thrones could also include the apostle Paul, Elijah, Enoch, Moses, John the Baptist, King David, Daniel, Abraham, John Wesley, Martin Luther, Charles Finney, or other candidates. This could be; however, the Bible does not seem to say. Nor is it wise to speculate with a sense of certainty.

If we understand the relation between Matthew 24, Revelation 6 and 7, and related passages, we can then understand that those who are mentioned as having been martyred and are underneath the alter, who are given white robes, include the first person to be martyred to those martyred until at least approximately 1914, found in Rev. 6:9-11. In Rev. 6:11, "... fellow servants and their brethren who were to be killed ..." (NASB), are likely those who have been killed for their faith since approximately 1914 and until the rapture, which includes many of us alive today.

We who are Christians on earth today are living with those mentioned in Revelation 6:10–11. If they are correct who say that the Church—the entire Church—has already been raptured in Revelation 6:10–11, then we are in big trouble, as the rapture would have already occurred. Have you heard of an extremely large number of people who suddenly vanished off the face of the earth? No. Therefore, those who have been preaching and teaching that the church is not mentioned after Revelation chapter 3 or 4 are gravely mistaken.

There is no passage in the Bible that says, "If you see twenty-four elders sitting on thrones in heaven in white robes, with crowns on their heads, then know that they are Christians who have been raptured into heaven." Which means this teaching was most likely an assumption.

My intent is not to be critical; the point is to be very clear about the truth. Why make this such an important issue? This is so important that a warning is given in the book of Revelation itself: "I testify to everyone who hears the words of the prophecy of this book: if anyone adds to them, God shall add to him the plagues which are written in this book; 19 and if anyone takes away from the words of the book of this prophecy, God shall take away his part from the tree of life and from the holy city, which are written in this book." (Rev.22:18-19, NASB).

It sounds as though anyone who adds to the book will have to go through the sufferings of the Great Tribulation. That would be a way of adding the plagues to that individual. It sounds as though anyone who takes away anything from the book of Revelation will lose his or her eternal salvation. This is the reason for the fuss: to let pastors who are mistakenly teaching this, know their error, understand the consequences, and recant.

It sounds as though there are few if any Christians on earth after the rapture. The only Christians who are not raptured are likely the 144,000 Messianic Jews who proclaim the gospel during the last part of the Great Tribulation, unless those adding or taking from God's word are included. If events in the book of Revelation are occurring in order, as they seem to be, those in Revelation 4:4 were not raptured, unless it is a matter of heaven being timeless. How could it be that Christians are not mentioned in the book of Revelation after Chapter 4, when they or actually we, are those of us who are now Christians, are mentioned in Revelation 6:11.

Whatever the consequences are exactly, it sounds risky even to write a book involving the book of Revelation. Most who have interpreted Revelation to say the Church is in heaven after chapter 4 must have intended good. God will surely take that into account yet the penalty may still apply.

Please research this for your own sake. Please consider giving a heads up to anyone who teaches this, in that way saving them a lot of grief. They should thank you.

11   The Perpetrator or Instigator

To gain more clarity, we need to go to what might seem to be an unlikely link to prophecy.

"Now there was a day when the sons of God came to present themselves before the Lord, and **Satan also came among them**. 7 And the Lord said to Satan, "From where do you come?" Then Satan answered the Lord and said, "From roaming about on the earth and walking around on it." 8 And the Lord said to Satan, "Have you considered My servant Job? For there is no one like him on the earth, a blameless and upright man, fearing God and turning away from evil." 9 Then Satan answered the Lord, "Does Job fear God for nothing? 10 "**Hast Thou not made a hedge about him** and his house and all that he has, on every side? Thou hast blessed the work of his hands, and his possessions have increased in the land. 11 "But put forth Thy hand now and touch all that he has: he will surely curse Thee to Thy face." 12 **Then the Lord said to Satan, "Behold, all that he has is in your power, only do not put forth your hand on him,"** So Satan departed from the presence of the Lord." (Job 1:6–12, NASB, EM).

Regarding verse six, I personally doubt that these people knew that they were presented before God, unless it was by their attendance on a Sabbath or a High Holy day, thereby thinking of themselves being presented before God. In verse 12, God allows Satan to destroy or take Job's possessions and kill some of his servants, but did not allow Satan to touch Job. God allowed certain things and set a limit at the same time.

"Now it happened on the day when his sons and his daughters were eating and drinking wine in their oldest brother's house, 14 that a messenger came to Job and said "'The oxen were plowing and the donkeys feeding beside them, 15 and **the Sabeans attacked and took them. They also slew the servants with the edge of the sword, and I alone have escaped to tell you."** 16 While he was still speaking, another also came and said, "**The fire of God fell from heaven and burned up the sheep and the servants and consumed them, and I alone have escaped to tell you."** 17 While he was still speaking, another also came and said, "**The Chaldeans formed three bands and made a raid on the camels and took them and slew the servants with the edge of the sword; and I alone have escaped to tell you.**" 18 While he was still speaking, another came and said, "**Your sons and your daughters were eating and drinking wine in their oldest brother's house, 19 and behold, a great wind came from across the wilderness and struck the four corners of the house, and it fell on the young people and they died; and I alone have escaped to tell you.**" 20 Then Job arose and tore his robe and shaved his head, and he fell to the ground and worshiped. 21 And he said, "Naked I came from my mother's womb, and naked I shall return there. The Lord gave and the Lord has taken away. Blessed be the name of the Lord." 22 Through all this Job did not sin nor did he blame God." (Job 1:13-22, NASB, EM).

Job 2:1 "Again there was a day when the sons of God came to present themselves before the Lord, and **Satan also came among them** to present himself before the Lord. 2 And the Lord said to Satan, "Where have you come from?" Then Satan answered the Lord and said, "From roaming about on the earth, and walking around on it." 3 And the Lord said to Satan, "Have you considered My servant Job? For there is no one like him on the earth, a blameless and upright man fearing God and turning away from evil. And he still holds fast his integrity, although you incited Me against him, to ruin him without cause." 4 **And Satan answered the Lord and said, "Skin for skin! Yes, all that** man **has he will give for his life. 5** "**However, put forth Thy hand, now, and touch his bone and his flesh; he will curse Thee to Thy face." 6 So the Lord said to Satan, "Behold, he is in your power, only spare his life." 7 Then Satan went out** from the presence of the Lord, **and smote Job with sore boils from the sole of his foot to the crown of his head."** (Job 2:1-7, NASB, EM).

Again God allowed Satan to cause Job pain, yet set a limit. Satan was not permitted to kill Job. "**And the Lord restored the fortunes of Job when he prayed for his friends, and the Lord increased all that Job had twofold.**" (Job 42:10, NASB, EM). God then blessed Job it seems for praying for his friends and for putting his faith, trust, and loyalty in God.

Compare Job chapters 1&2 with what is occurring in Revelation 6: "And I looked, and behold, a white horse, and he who sat on it had a bow; and **a crown was given to him; and he went out conquering, and to conquer.**" (Rev. 6:2, NASB, EM).

Here God is almost certainly giving this crown—allowing Satan to instigate false Christianity, just as Satan asked to cause Job suffering. There is no mention of a limit, yet a limit was likely set.

"And another, a red horse, went out; **and to him who sat on it, <u>it was granted</u> to take peace from the earth, and that *men* should slay one another; and <u>a great sword was given</u> to him**." (Rev. 6:4, NASB, EM). Again God has granted—allowed—that "men should slay one another," and that Satan will carry this out. The passage says, "It was granted" (allowed). Who asked for the power? Now think of World War I, World War II, War in North Korea, Vietnam, Iraq, Afghanistan, and other wars. Who instigated these?

"And I heard as it were a voice in the center of the four living creatures saying, "**A quart of wheat <u>for a denarius</u>, and three quarts of barley <u>for a denarius</u>; and <u>do not harm the oil and the wine.</u>**" (Rev. 6:6, NASB, EM). The amount of grain for a denarius—a day's wage—was a limit of cost set by God. Another limit was set when he said, "do not harm the oil and the wine." God has almost certainly set a limit on how bad the famine will be and limited Satan, who is behind it. Consider the famines from approximately 1914 through today and the Great Tribulation, with Satan behind them.

"And I looked, and behold, an ashen horse; and he who sat on it had the name Death; and Hades was following with him. And **<u>authority was given</u> to them <u>over a fourth of the earth</u>, to kill with sword and with famine and with pestilence and by the wild beasts of the earth.**" (Rev. 6:8, NASB, EM). It is very clear that "authority was given," so it must be God allowing this. Why? To produce repentance. A limit to these calamities is set so as not to affect more than a fourth of the earth. Who was the authority given to? Again, Satan is almost certainly the instigator or, in a sense, the perpetrator.

"And there was given to each of them a white robe; and they were told that they should rest for a little while longer, **until the number** of **their fellow servants** and their **brethren who were to be killed** even as they had been, **should be completed also**." (Rev. 6:11, NASB, EM). "Until the number"—it is almost certain that there has been a specific number set, as a limit to be killed. "Who were to be killed" were qualified as Christians to be martyred for their faith. "Should be completed"—again God is setting a limit to the number of his people Satan is allowed to martyr.

Some people may be upset that God would allow any of these things. Some of these things seem to be allowed to test our faith, as Job was tested. It is as though God is saying, "Your heart needs to be proven, tested like Job." Not proven to God, as He knows our heart, but proven as in evidence for proof in a trial. This is the case of Job, whom God seems to be proud of: "my servant Job" (NASB); and "there is no one on earth like him" (NASB).

It sounds like God is enjoying Job's commitment to Him, as some young men enjoy receiving a great sports car and want to test it out. (Caution: don't do it.)

God allows these things as an opportunity, as a witness to bring others to Christ. In addition it is likely that these things occur as a warning to repent, obey God. As noted, these events occur to a large extent due to Satan, since most of society has ignored or is opposed to God's Word. Much of the world has, without considering it, been embracing a spirit of Antichrist.

Revelation starts by saying that the book is a revelation from Christ. Then we are told about letters to seven Churches, and then the "Great Tribulation" and the time leading to it.

In the letter to the Church at Smyrna, Christ says, "'Do not fear what you are about to suffer. Behold, the devil is about to cast some of you into prison, that you may be tested, …" (Rev.2:10, NASB). This seems to be more confirmation that Satan is behind the events of the five seals, false Christs, wars, famine, and martyrdom.

Therefore it would seem that those who are not following God are and will be experiencing suffering because they have followed Satan's path. These sufferings are an opportunity to live our lives in a way that will glorify Christ, in a way that will encourage other Christians and bring others to Christ.

Be careful not to let what God allows upset you. "Woe to the one who quarrels with his Maker--…" (Isa. 45:9, NASB). God restored to Job after His trial, as Job was found to be upright. May it be the same for you.

A Brief Recap

Daniel 12:4 refers to "the end of the age"—the latter part of the Industrial Age and the Information Age. Jesus refers to things that occur during the time Daniel mentions and the generation that sees Israel spring back to life in 1948. This gives us an approximate overall idea of the time of "the end of the age," of the end times, which seem to end by approximately 2028 to 2031. During this period so far, there have been wars, famines, earthquakes, epidemics, and false Christs—the white horse. All of these seem to be escalating, giving evidence of birth pangs—the ashen horse.

Return to the Ashen Horse

We looked at the first two chapters of Job, with Satan's request and God's response. Then we compared that with passages in Revelation 6, noting the similarity of things allowed and limitations made. This indicates that Satan, to a large degree, is behind the false Christs, war, famine, pestilence and martyrdom. Now seems the appropriate time to give another reason to think that Satan is behind the ashen horse.

Please note what occurs in Revelation 6:8: "And I looked, and behold, an ashen horse; and **he who sat on it** had the **name Death; and Hades** was following with **him**. And authority was given …" (NASB, EM). There is one more passage to compare these statements with, involving a completely different white horse.

"And I saw heaven opened; and behold, a white horse, and He who sat upon it *is* called Faithful and True; and in righteousness He Judges and wages war ... 13 And He *is* clothed with a robe dipped in blood; and His name is called The Word of God. ... 16 And on His robe and on His thigh He has a name written, "KING OF KINGS, AND LORD OF LORDS." ... 20:14 And **death and Hades** were thrown into the lake of fire. This is the **second death**, the lake of fire." (Rev. 19:11, 13, 16, 20:14, NASB, EM). Here "Death and Hades" are being "thrown into the lake of fire"; this is Satan. Satan is behind the ashen horse. The ashen horse has the same attribute or name, "Death; and Hades"—Satan.

Has the World Gone Crazy?

I hope you already have one idea of why it seems to many that the world has gone crazy: Satan has been working to instigate delusional thinking, hate, and behavior which violates God's word. No matter what your beliefs or political persuasion, people likely appear to be more illogical. "I say this in order that no one may delude you with persuasive argument." (Col. 2:4, NASB).

When people hear what they want to hear—that they don't have to work, that they can live a life of hedonism, that college, housing, food, and health care are free because someone else will pay for them—many will embrace it, and many have enthusiastically embraced it. The government is much bigger than us all; why can't the government just pay for it? "But prove yourselves doers of the word, and not merely hearers who delude themselves." (James 1:22, NASB). The government receives all of its money from the taxpayers, and our money is limited.

12   The Blood Moons

"…and the sun became black as sackcloth *made* of hair, and the whole moon became like blood;" (Rev. 6:12, NASB)

This passage and others are talking about the same event or events—almost certainly a series of four blood moons and solar eclipses—though described just a bit differently. These blood moons need to be understood to gain an overall picture of what is happening. Mark Blitz may have been first to notice these uncommon blood moon sets. (www.elshaddaiministries. us) 3/28/2016.[1]

Blood moons and solar eclipses have been observed since humans have been on earth. The NASA has calculated when blood moons and solar eclipses will occur for decades.

For those not familiar with a blood moon, it is similar to a total eclipse of the sun, which happens when the moon's orbit moves between the sun and the earth. When this occurs, most of the sunlight is blocked from reaching the earth. The sunlight that is seen during a total eclipse of the sun is the outermost part of the sun, called the corona.

With a blood moon, the earth's orbit brings the earth between the sun and the moon. The earth blocks almost all sunlight from reaching the moon. The small amount of light reaching the moon comes through earth's atmosphere, which gives the moon an orange glow, or a pinkish or reddish look. So the phenomenon is called a blood moon. Blood moons and solar eclipses can be seen only from certain places on earth. The location changes from blood moon to blood moon and with each solar eclipse.

There is no need to try the following. It is only intended to provide a mental comparison to a blood moon.

Imagine that some people found a dark gymnasium to use. They hung a basketball by a string near the center of the court. Someone then pointed a bright red light (representing the sun) at that basketball from about forty feet away. Then someone held a baseball, representing the moon, also by a string.

The baseball would be centered on the dark side of the basketball, the side that does not have the red light shining on it. The person holding the baseball would slowly walk away from the basketball, which is also being carried away from the bright red light. While walking away, the baseball holder would try to keep the baseball completely out of the light.

For someone standing just beside the baseball, there would be a point at perhaps twenty or fifty feet away from the basketball where only the very outer edges of the baseball have a bit of red light on them. This gives a general idea of what is happening during a blood moon.

Someone may tell you, "Oh, but there of plenty of blood moons; a blood moon is not an unusual event." True, but that is not the context. There will be about 230 blood moons this century, from 2000 till 2100. From 1400 through 2099, there have been and will be approximately 1,921 blood moons. https:/en;Wikipedia.org/wiki/Lists_of_lunar_eclipses 3/28/2016 https:/en,Wikipedia.org/wiki/Lunar_eclipse 3/28/2016

https://en.wikipedia.org/Lists_of_solar_eclipses 3/28/2016[2]

We are not talking about just blood moons, but blood moons accompanying exceptional historic Jewish events during two specific Jewish High Holy days. This is not as improbable as the cosmological fine tuning, yet still improbable enough to attract attention. Four sets of four blood moons and two solar eclipses—in 1492–1493, 1948–1949, 1967–1968, were accompanied by important historical Jewish events. The events of the 2014-2015 blood moons will be explained.

First, we are talking about sets of four blood moons, so we divide 1,921 by 4, equaling approximately 480.25 sets of four. Of all these blood moon sets called tirades, there seem to be only four sets of four blood moons with solar eclipses, which occurred during Jewish High Holy Days of Nisan and Sukkot, during which important historical events involving God's chosen people occurred, from 1400 through 1967. According to Joel 2:31, the event (stars falling from the sky--fire and brimstone) associated with the 2014-2015 blood moon set comes after that blood moon set occurs.

In 1492, Jews were being forced out of Spain. A set of four blood moons occurred, two in 1493. One blood moon occurred on April 16, during or near Passover, and the other on October 10, on or near Sukkoth.

In 1948, the Jews returned to Israel. Instead of the more common two blood moons per year, there were a total of four blood moons. These blood moons occurred on March 6th, April 5th, August 30[th,] and September 29th. Of the two blood moons in 1949, one occurred on April 17, during Passover, which ran from April 14 through April 20. The other blood moon came on October 15, during Sukkoth, which ran from October 8th through October 14.

In 1967, Israel fought the Six Day War against an alliance of Arab countries. In 1968, one blood moon came on April 16, during Passover, which ran from April 13 through April 19. The other came on October 9, during Sukkoth, which ran from October 7 through October 13.

Four unusual sets (including the 2014–2015 set) out of 480 possible sets, or one set in every 120, is less than 1 percent. This definitely sets them apart from typical blood moon sets. In light of these specific conditions, no, these blood moons are not common.

Pastor John Hagee's research on blood moons led to his sermon "The Coming Four Blood Moons."[3] Pastor Hagee brought to light the blood moons that occurred in 1492, 1948, 1967, and 2014-2015, and he speaks of the accompanying Jewish High Holy days and historic events. See Pastor Hagee's sermon at (tellmessage.blogspot.com.) You can also access more of Pastor Hagee's resources at (jhm.org) 3/28/2016 and (www. faithcenteredresources.com/). 3/28/2016

The likelihood that two of the most historic Jewish events in history have occurred during this period from 1914 to 2025 and have coincided with four blood moons sequences and been accompanied by Jewish High Holy Days is unlikely.

People who say these blood moon sets are not unusual must not have known about the accompanying events during these specific blood moons, or perhaps don't care. Common sense teaches us about probability. You seldom find a bag of one-hundred-dollar bills lying on the street.

13   Revelation Chapter Six

"And I saw when the Lamb broke one of the seven seals, and I heard one of the four living creatures saying as with a voice of thunder, "Come." 2 And I looked, and behold, a white horse, and he who sat on it had a bow; and a crown was given to him; and he went out conquering, and to conquer. 3 And when He broke the second seal, I heard the second living creature saying, "Come." 4 And another, a red horse, went out; and to him who sat on it, it was granted to take peace from the earth, and that *men* should slay one another; and a great sword was given to him. 5 And when He broke the third seal, I heard the third living creature saying, "Come." And I looked, and behold, a black horse; and he who sat on it had a pair of scales in his hand. 6 And I heard as it were a voice in the center of the four living creatures saying, "A quart of wheat for a denarius, and three quarts of barley for a denarius; and do not harm the oil and the wine." 7 And when He broke the fourth seal, I heard the voice of the fourth living creature saying, "Come." 8 And I looked, and behold, an ashen horse; and he who sat on it had the name Death; and Hades was following with him. And authority was given to them over a fourth of the earth, to kill with sword and with famine and with pestilence and by the wild beasts of the earth. 9 And when He broke the fifth seal, I saw underneath the altar the souls of those who had been slain because of the word of God, and because of the testimony which they had maintained; 10 and they cried out with a loud voice, saying, "How long, O Lord, holy and true, wilt Thou refrain from judging and avenging our blood on those who dwell on the earth?" 11 And there was given to each of them a white robe; and they were told that they should rest for a little while longer, until *the number of* their fellow servants and their brethren who were to be killed even as they had been, should be completed also. 12 And I looked when He broke the sixth seal, and there was a great earthquake; and the sun became black as sackcloth *made* of hair, and the whole moon became like blood; 13 and the stars of the sky fell to the earth, as a fig tree casts its unripe figs when shaken by a great wind. 14 And the sky was split apart like a scroll when it is rolled up; and every mountain and island were moved out of their places. 15 And the kings of the earth and the great men and the commanders and the rich and the strong and every slave and free man, hid themselves in the caves and among the rocks of the mountains; 16 and they said to the mountains and to the rocks, "Fall on us and hide us from the presence of Him who sits on the throne, and from the wrath of the Lamb; 17 for the great day of their wrath has come; and who is able to stand?" (Rev. 6:1–17, NASB).

14   The Sixth Seal: Hang On

In the last half of Revelation 6, there are a few things occurring in close succession. There are two events that may be occurring within perhaps thirty minutes or possibly a second of each other.

"And I looked when He broke the sixth seal, and there was a great earthquake; and **the sun became black as sackcloth** *made* **of hair, and the whole moon became like blood;**" (Rev. 6:12, NASB, EM).

"But immediately after the tribulation of those days **THE SUN WILL BE DARKENED, AND THE MOON WILL NOT GIVE ITS LIGHT, …**" (Matt. 24:29, NASB, EM).

Revelation 6:12 and Matthew 24:29 are describing the same events. In both cases, sunlight normally reflecting off the moon's surface is not shining—"the moon will not give its light"—since the earth is blocking almost all of the light. The moon has a blood—pink, red, or orange—hue. The whole moon becomes like blood. This is almost certainly referring to a lunar eclipse as seen from earth. These blood moons are coming in sets months apart, accompanied by two solar eclipses. The solar eclipse, of course, happens when the moon obstructs the light of the sun as it moves between the earth and the sun—"The sun will be darkened."

Could God be speaking of a different miraculous event instead of these unique solar and lunar eclipses? That is possible. However, these specific blood moon events are unlikely and very timely. The descriptions in Revelation 6 sound so apocalyptic, so frightening, that the blood moons might seem to be something never seen before. Yet note the wars, famine, and martyrs are things mentioned in Revelation 6 that have been seen in the past from time to time. However, these wars are now much worse and impact more people. The blood moons are unique, and three sets occur during the time period mentioned by Jesus.

Why should the moon turning to blood have to be an event never seen before, instead of something people are generally familiar with, yet unique? If the descriptions of the moon turning to blood were not astronomical phenomenon but unexplainable miraculous events, then the return of the Lord might not come as a thief in the night for anyone. The blood moons seem to be the fulfillment of the revelation of John in Revelation 6.

Only people living in certain locations, looking at the correct time, saw these blood moons, and only in specific locations did they see total lunar eclipses. Revelation 6 and Matthew 24 are again stating the same thing. If you accept this, there are now six topics in a row of Revelation 6 and Matthew 24 expressing the same ideas, with a skip, which will be explained

God's Wrath

"and the **stars of the sky fell to the earth,** as a fig tree casts its unripe figs when shaken by a great wind. …17 for the **great day of their wrath has come**; …" (Rev. 6:13, 17 NASB, EM).

"**…AND THE STARS WILL FALL** from the sky, and the powers of the heavens will be shaken," (Matt. 24:29, NASB, EM).

Revelation 6 and Matthew 24 are again saying the same thing. These "stars" cannot, of course, be actual stars, as stars are extremely large and just one would destroy earth. However, shooting stars—meteors and meteorites burning as they fall through earth's atmosphere—fit the description well. This is likely what occurred in Sodom and Gomorra (Gen. 19:24). Jesus, "it was the same as happened in the days of Lot;…29…it rained fire and brimstone …"(Luke 17:28&29, NASB). There are now seven subjects, in the same order in Revelation 6 and Matthew 24.

Christ's Return, Christ Is Seen

"And **the sky was split apart like a scroll when it is rolled up**; and every mountain and island were moved out of their places." (Rev. 6:14, NASB, EM).

"and they said to the mountains and to the rocks, "Fall on us and hide us **from the presence of Him who sits on the throne, and from the wrath of the Lamb;**" (Rev. 6:16, NASB, EM).

"For just as the lightning comes from the east, and flashes even to the west, so shall the coming of the Son of Man be." (Matt. 24:27, NASB).

"and then the **sign of the Son of Man will appear in the sky**, and then all the tribes of the earth will mourn, and they will **see the Son of Man** COMING ON THE CLOUDS OF THE SKY with power and great glory." (Matt. 24:30, NASB, EM).

Although it may not be obvious, Christ the Lamb has just appeared in the sky. The phrases "the sky was split apart like a scroll," "hide us from the presence of Him who sits on the throne," and "the sign of the Son of Man will appear in the sky" are describing Christ's return. Like the curtain on a stage being pulled back, revealing those on stage, perhaps the very fabric of space, as scientists refer to it, is peeled back revealing another realm and Christ.

"Oh, that Thou wouldst rend the heavens and come down, that the mountains might quake at Thy presence … 3 … Thou didst come down, the mountains quaked at Thy presence-" (Isa. 64:1, 3, NASB). *Rend*, of course, means to rip or tear apart. This passage from Isaiah likely describes the same event, the rapture.

For those of you who agree that these match, there is now an eighth parallel between Revelation 6 and Matthew 24. You may wish to question whether this point is in order. If you read through this a few times, you may notice that it is all tied in together so closely that it may seem a bit difficult to separate in time.

A few verses may help clear up questions:

"And after He had said these things, He was lifted up while they were looking on, and a cloud received Him out of their sight. 10 And as they were gazing intently into the sky while He was departing, behold, two men in white clothing stood beside them; 11 and they also said, "Men of Galilee, why do you stand looking into the sky? This Jesus, who has been taken up from you into heaven, will come in just the same way as you have watched Him go into heaven.'" (Acts 1:9–11, NASB).

"BEHOLD, HE IS COMING WITH THE CLOUDS, and **every eye will see Him**, even those who pierced Him; and all the tribes of the earth will mourn over Him. Even so, Amen." (Rev. 1:7, NASB).

"For the Lord Himself will descend from heaven with a shout, with the voice of the archangel, and with the trumpet of God; and the dead in Christ shall rise first. 17 Then we who are alive and remain shall be caught up together with them in the clouds to meet the Lord in the air, and thus we shall always be with the Lord." (1 Thess. 4:16–17, NASB).

Yes, this is almost certainly the rapture, with eight parallels in which Matthew 24 and Revelation agree, and perhaps all in the same order. Revelation 1:7 says "even those who pierced Him" (NASB) will see Christ. Even those who crucified Christ and thrust a spear into His side (John 19:34).

Tribes Mourn

"And the kings of the earth and the great men and the commanders and the rich and the strong and every slave and free man, **hid themselves in the caves and among the rocks of the mountains; 16 and <u>they said to the mountains and to the rocks, "Fall on us and hide us from the presence of Him who sits on the throne, and from the *wrath* of the Lamb; 17 for the great day of their *wrath* has come; and who is able to stand</u>?" (Rev. 6:15–17, NASB, EM).

"and then the sign of the Son of Man will appear in the sky, and then **all the tribes of the earth will mourn,** and they will see the SON of MAN COMING ON THE CLOUDS OF THE SKY with power and great glory." (Matt. 24:30, NASB, EM).

All the tribes—all the people on earth—are mourning, complaining about God's wrath. Unfortunately, they are almost definitely not mourning their sin. They are mourning, complaining and moaning because of the suffering being poured out. God is releasing His wrath, and the stars are falling from the sky—fire and brimstone—likely meteorites falling on their heads. Some of these falling stars are possibly the size of a baseball and could destroy a car due to their speed. Others, perhaps the size of a pebble by the time they reach the ground, could kill or seriously wound. The Lord's wrath is mentioned in Revelation 6:16 and 6:17.

The mourning found in Revelation 6:15, the statements "hide us" and "who is able to stand"(NASB), are comments of those experiencing God's wrath—both are cries of mourning. In Matthew 24:30, "all the tribes of the earth will mourn" (NASB). In both cases, they are complaining about God's wrath.

If you accept that Revelation 6:16,17 and Matthew 24:30 speak of nonbelievers mourning the wrath of God, then there is a ninth parallel between Revelation 6 and Matthew 24.

Someone might say, did the apostle John make this up?" Again, remember. Jesus's disciples were being martyred at the time John wrote. Whether they were crucified as Christ was or murdered in some other way, they were being killed for what they believed. If you believe in Christ so strongly that you would rather be crucified than deny your faith in Jesus, why would you fabricate Revelation 6? Even today, ISIS is beheading Christians—not with a guillotine, but by the use of a knife, sword or axe—if Christians will not deny Christ.

15 Is This a Pre–Great Tribulation Rapture? Seven to Ten Reasons

It sounds like a pre-tribulation rapture. After all, Paul said in 1 Thessalonians 5:9, "For God has not destined us for wrath, but for obtaining salvation through our Lord Jesus Christ," (NASB).

"For the Lord Himself will descend …" (1 Thess. 4:16, NASB).

"…The Son of Man will appear in the sky, … see the Son of Man COMING ON THE CLOUDS …" (Matt. 24:30, (NASB).

"…This Jesus, who has been taken up from you into heaven, will come in just the same way as you have watched Him go into heaven, …" (Acts 1:11, NASB).

"…THEY WILL GATHER TOGETHER HIS elect …" (Matt.24:31, NASB).

The rapture and then wrath. However, is this really a pre-tribulation rapture? On to Revelation 7.

"After this I saw four angels standing at the four corners of the earth, holding back the four winds of the earth, so that no wind should blow on the earth or on the sea or on any tree. 2 And I saw another angel ascending from the rising of the sun, having the seal of the living God; and he cried out with a loud voice to the **four angels to whom it was granted to harm the earth and the sea, 3 saying, "Do not harm the earth or the sea or the trees, until we have sealed the bond-servants of our God on their foreheads,"** 4 And I heard the number of those who were sealed, one hundred and forty-four thousand sealed from every tribe of the sons of Israel: 5 from the tribe of Judah twelve thousand were sealed, from the tribe of Ruben twelve thousand, from the tribe of Gad twelve thousand, 6 from the tribe of Asher twelve thousand, from the tribe of Naphtali twelve thousand, from the tribe of Manasseh twelve thousand, 7 from the tribe of Simeon twelve thousand, from the tribe of Levi twelve thousand, from the tribe of Issachar twelve thousand, 8 from the tribe of Zebulun twelve thousand, from the tribe of Joseph twelve thousand, from the tribe of Benjamin, twelve thousand were sealed." (Rev.7:1-8, NASB, EM).

Whether a pre-tribulation, mid-tribulation, or post-tribulation rapture, the rapture has almost certainly occurred soon before God's wrath, or at the same time as these 144,000 are sealed. In Revelation 7:3–7, those mentioned come from the twelve tribes of Israel, so they are Jews. They are almost certainly being sealed for their protection during the Great Tribulation.

These 144,000 Jews who have been sealed will witness during the "Great Tribulation." The question is, witness during the first half, the last half, or all of the Great Tribulation? This should become clear.

"After these things I looked, and behold, **a great multitude, which no one could count, from every nation and all tribes and peoples and tongues, standing before the throne and before the Lamb, clothed in white robes, and palm branches were in their hands;** 10 and they cry out with a loud voice, saying "Salvation to our God who sits on the throne, and to the Lamb."11 And all the angels were standing around the throne and around the elders and the four living creatures; and they fell on their faces before the throne and worshiped God, 12 saying, "Amen, blessing, and glory and wisdom and thanksgiving and honor and power and might, be to our God forever and ever. Amen." (Rev. 7:9-12, NASB, EM).

Fantastic! All these Christians are in heaven, with white robes. Just about eleven verses earlier in Revelation, the passages talked about the rapture and the time just before the rapture. This is almost certainly refers to people who were raptured in Matthew 24:27–31. It still sounds like a pre-tribulation rapture. Revelation continues.

The <u>FIRST</u> strong proof that it will be a mid-tribulation rapture occurs in Revelation 7:13–14: "And one of the elders answered, saying to me, **"These who are clothed in white robes, who are they, and from where have they come?"** 14 And I said to him, "My lord, you know." And he said to me, **"These are the ones who come <u>out of the great tribulation,</u>**

and they have washed their robes and made them white in the blood of the Lamb." (NASB, EM).

What happened? The phrase "out of" in the Greek means out of the middle of or out of the midst of. Yes, as in out of the middle of the Great Tribulation, out of the midst of it. Yet it had sounded like a pre-tribulation rapture. Yet this seems to clearly state that it is a mid-tribulation rapture. This is the first strong indicator of a mid-tribulation rapture.

Are there any other ways to confirm or deny this? Yes. We know that Revelation 6 and Matthew 24 have the same content in the same order, except that Revelation 6 is just a bit shorter. If we put these two chapters side by side, it may help us to understand.

The next three pages will be "The Second Parallel View." The intent is for you to read a couple of verses in the left column, then a couple of verses in the right column, to see how they compare. To relieve any confusion, note that Revelation 6 skips 20 verses in Matthew 24. It is important to notice what Revelation 6 skips over.

Again, you may want to use a highlighter, perhaps a bright yellow one, to underline every time you see the words "then," "after," "those days," and "not yet the end." The Guide for the "Second Parallel View" follows bellow.

1   False Christs and false teaching; in Matt.24:4-5 and Rev.6:2, 8.
2   War; in Matt.24:5 and Rev.6:4
3   Famine; in Matt.24:7 and Rev.6:5-6,8
4   Suffering Increases; in Matt.24:8 Birth Pangs and in Rev.6:8 the ashen horse.
5   Martyrdom; in Matt.24:9 and Rev.6:9-11
6   Blood Moons; in Matt.24:29 and Rev 6:12
7   Christ Seen - the Rapture; in Matt.24:27,28,30 and Rev.6:16,17
8   Stars Fall; in Matt.24:2 and Rev.6:13
9   Tribes Mourn; in Matt.24:30 and Rev.6:16,17
10 God's Wrath; in Rev.616,17 and Matt.24:29
    Timing; when-Matt.24:3. The sequence – Then and then and then-Matt.24:9,14,16,21,23,30

The Second Parallel View

Matthew 24:3 " …Tell us, **when will these things be**, and **what will be the sign of Your coming,** and of **the end of the age**?" 4 And Jesus answered and said to them, **"See to it that no one misleads you. 5 "For many will come in My name, saying, 'I am the Christ,'** and **will mislead many.** 6 "And you will **be hearing of wars and rumors of wars;** see that you are not frightened, for *those things* must take place, but that is not yet the end. 7 For nation will rise against nation, and kingdom against kingdom, and in various places there will be **famines** and earthquakes." (NASB, EM).

Matthew 24:8 "But all these things are *merely* **the beginning of birth pangs."** (NASB, EM)

Rev. 6:2 "And I looked, and behold, a **white horse**, and he who sat on it had **a bow**; and **a crown** *was given* to him; and he went out **conquering, and to conquer.** 3 And when He broke the second seal, I heard the second living creature saying, "Come." 4 And another, a **red horse**, went out; and to him who sat on it, *it was granted* **to take peace from the earth**, and that *men* **should slay one another**; and a **great sword** *was given to him.* 5 And when He broke the third seal, I heard the third living creature saying, "Come." And I looked, and behold, a **black horse**; and he who sat on it had a **pair of scales** in his hand." 6… **"A quart of wheat for a denarius, and three quarts of barley for a denarius**; and *do not harm the oil and the wine."*… 8 And I looked, and behold, **an ashen horse;** and he who sat on it had the name **Death**; and **Hades was following** with him. And *authority was given to them* over a *fourth of the earth,* **to kill with sword and with famine** and with **pestilence** and **by the wild beasts of the earth.** 9 And when He broke the fifth seal, I saw underneath the altar the souls of those who had been slain because of the word of God, and because of the testimony which they had maintained;"(NASB, EM)

Matthew 24:9 "**Then** they will deliver you to tribulation, and **will kill you**, and you will be hated by all nations **on account of My name**. 10 "And **at that time** many will fall away and will deliver up one another and hate one another. 11 "And many false prophets will arise, and will mislead many. 12 "And because lawlessness is increased, most people's love will grow cold. 13 "But the one who endures to the end, he shall be saved. 14 "And this gospel of the kingdom shall be preached in the whole world for a witness to all the nations, and **then the end shall come**. 15 "Therefore **when** you see the ABOMINATION OF DESOLATION which was spoken of through Daniel the prophet, standing in the holy place (let the reader understand), 16 **then** let those who are in Judea flee to the mountains; 17 let him who is on the housetop not go down to get the things out that are in his house; 18 and let him who is in the field not turn back to get his cloak. 19 "But woe to those who are with child and to those who nurse babes in those days! 20 "But pray that your flight may not be in the winter, or on a Sabbath; 21 for **then** there will be a **great tribulation**, such as has not occurred since the beginning of the world until now, nor ever shall." (NASB, EM).

Revelation 6:10 and they cried out with a loud voice, saying, "How long, O Lord, holy and true, wilt Thou refrain from judging and avenging our blood on those who dwell on the earth?" 11 And there was given to each of them a <u>white robe</u>; and they were told that they should rest for a little while longer, *until the number* of their **fellow servants** and **their brethren who were to be killed** even as they had been, *should be completed also.*" (NASB, EM).

[Revelation 6:11 parallels with Matthew 24:9. Now Revelation chapter 6 skips all the way to Matthew 24:29. What does it skip? The first half of the Great Tribulation.]

[It would be good to read Matthew 24:10, which starts near the top of the left-hand column, through Matthew 24:28 and see what Revelation chapter 6 skips over.]

Matthew 24:22 "And unless those days had been cut short, no life would have been saved; but for the sake of the elect those days shall be cut short. 23 "**Then** if anyone says to you, 'Behold, here is the Christ,' or 'There He is,' do not believe him. 24 "For false Christs and false prophets will arise and will show great signs and wonders, so as to mislead, if possible, even the elect.25 "Behold, I have told you in advance. 26 "If therefore they say to you, 'Behold, He is in the wilderness,' ... 27 "For just as lightning comes from the east, and flashes even to the west, so shall the <u>coming of the Son of Man</u> be. 28 "Wherever the corpse is, there the vultures will gather. 29 "But immediately **after** *the tribulation of* **those days THE SUN WILL BE DARKENED, AND THE MOON WILL NOT GIVE ITS LIGHT, AND THE STARS WILL FALL** from the sky, and the powers of the heavens will be shaken, 30 and **then** the sign of the Son of Man will appear in the sky, and **then all the tribes of the earth will mourn**, and <u>they will see the SON OF MAN COMING ON THE CLOUDS OF THE SKY</u> with power and great glory." (NASB, EM).

[Revelation chapter 6 skips over the first portion of the Great Tribulation and skips to Christ's return for the Church at the rapture and the beginning of wrath to be poured out. Notice where Revelation picks up again.]

Revelation 6:12 "And I looked when He broke the sixth seal, and there was a great earthquake; and **the sun became black as sackcloth made of hair, and the whole moon became like blood;** 13 and the **stars of the sky fell to the earth,** as a fig tree casts its unripe figs when shaken by a great wind. ... 14 And the sky was split apart... 16 ... **"Fall on us and hide us from** <u>the presence of Him who sits on the throne,</u> **and from the wrath of** <u>the Lamb</u>**; 17 for the great day of** <u>their</u> **wrath has come; and who is able to stand?"** (NASB, EM). *[As you can see Rev. 6:12 picked up here after the "Great Tribulation" stated in Matthew 24:21.*

16 What Just Happened?

We can have great confidence that Revelation 7:9 tells us that the great multitude seen in heaven, is made up of those who have just been raptured. This "great multitude," those who are living in the time of the generation Christ mentioned—1914 through 2028 (approximately)—are raptured out of the Great Tribulation in the not too distant future. It may be helpful to have your Bible out to follow along with now.

The SECOND strong proof that it will be a mid-tribulation rapture. A comparison of Revelation chapter 6:12–13 to Matthew 24:15-26 shows us that Revelation 6 skips over the first half of the Great Tribulation. Revelation 6:9-11 mentions martyrdom, as does Matthew 24:9. Then Revelation 6:12, which speaks of the blood moons, picks up in Matthew 24:29 where the blood moons and stars falling from the sky are mentioned. Revelation chapter 6 has just skipped 20 verses in Matthew 24. The skip after Rev. 6:12 comes not long before (likely 7-14 years before) the first part of the Great Tribulation mentioned in Matthew 24:15-16. Revelation 6:13 then picks up as the first portion of the Great Tribulation has just ended with the rapture and then God's wrath begins, which are both mentioned in Matthew 24:27-30. This implies the first portion of the Great Tribulation occurs between Revelation 6:12 and 6:13. This reinforces the mid-tribulation concept.

Again, *mid-tribulation* means that Christians alive at the time go through the first part—half—of the Great Tribulation before they are raptured.

Now a Split Verse

In Revelation 6:12 & 13 the blood moons follow immediately after the martyrdom in Rev. 6:9-11. Our immediate thought might be that the blood moons, and then stars falling from the sky, occur immediately after the martyrdom of Rev. 9:-11. However the events in Revelation 6 and Matthew 24 have been occurring in the same sequence one after another. Revelation 6 skips over 20 verses, from Matt.24:9 and starts up again with the blood moons and stars falling from the sky in Matt. 24:29. Now it appears that the blood moons and the stars falling form the sky, occur after the Great Tribulation, which creates a problem. The blood moons occurred in 2014 – 2015 and stars did not fall from the sky. Does this mean the blood moons of 2014 – 2015 are not the event Christ was speaking of? Unlikely, the blood moons are almost certainly what Christ spoke of and further explanation is given in chapter 17. In Matt. 24:27, 28, 30 & 31 elements at the time of the rapture are mentioned before and after God's wrath – the stars falling from the sky in verse 29. Since the rapture happens, "…in the twinkling of an eye" (1Corr. 15:52, NASB), there would not be enough time for the two year period of the blood moons to pass. Is there anything in these verses that would give an explanation?

"But immediately **after** the tribulation of those days THE SUN WILL BE DARKENED, AND THE MOON WILL NOT GIVE ITS LIGHT, …" (Matt. 24:29, NASB, EM). This part of verse 29 does not say after the "Great Tribulation" but "after the tribulation of those days" (NASB, EM). Matthew 24:29 mentions just "tribulation" and "**after**," not "then."

The THIRD proof of a mid-tribulation rapture. Is there any verse in Matthew 24 which mentions just "tribulation" and not "Great Tribulation"? Yes. Matthew 24:9 uses just the word "tribulation," which tells us that the first half of Matthew 24:29 comes - occurs, just after Matthew 24:9 in time sequence, since it is "after" the "tribulation" of those days. Since Matthew 24 and Revelation 6 have been following the same order, Revelation 6:12 "… the sun became black as sackcloth made of hair, and the whole moon became like blood:" (NASB), remains in order after Rev. 6:9-11 – martyrdom. The second portion of Mat.24:29 which reads "…AND THE STARS WILL FALL from the sky, and the powers of the heavens will be shaken." (NASB) remains where it is in chronological order in verse 29. It then maintains its association with those suffering from these stars falling from the sky in Matt. 24:30. The order can be seen on page 83 & 104. Following the same order as Matthew 24, Revelation 6:13 "and the stars of the sky fell to the earth…" (NASB), (the same topic), also occurs at the same time as the stars falling from the sky in Matthew 24:29. This is the beginning of God's wrath, the second part of the Great Tribulation, which occurs very soon after the rapture. Matthew 24:27&28 refers to the rapture. Jesus uses the words "when" and "then" to indicate the order in which events occur. The phrase "coming of the Son of the Man" in Matt. 24:27 (NASB) is telling us that Jesus has returned in the sky just as Acts 1:10-11 says He will. Matt. 24:28 "Wherever the corpse is, there the vultures will gather." (NASB) This tells us that just as vultures search for the dead and then carry them away, angels will also search out Christians and gather them. The same concept is also mentioned again just five verses later. Matt. 24:31 "And He will send forth His angels with a GREAT TRUMPET and THEY WILL GATHER His elect from the four winds, from one end of the sky to the other." (NASB) The skip that Revelation 6:12–13 makes from Matthew 24:9, martyrdom, to Matthew 24:29, the blood moons, confirm this is a split verse-split by time. When this is done the same approximate 7 to 14 years pass in Matthew between the blood moon and stars falling from the sky, as in Rev. 6:12 to 13. Understanding that the first half of Matthew 24:29 comes immediately after Matthew 24:9 in time explains that the same jump in time occurs in Matthew 24 as in Revelation 6. Only when we place the first half of Matthew 24:29 after Matthew 24:9 (creating the correct order of events) do we then understand that the blood moons occur soon after the martyrdom of Matt. 24:9, not after the first portion of the Great Tribulation nor after the entire Great Tribulation.

Note, as the phrase in Matthew 24:29, "after the tribulation of <u>those days</u>," there is an almost identical phrase in Mark 13:24: "But in <u>those days</u>, <u>after that tribulation, …</u>" (NASB, EM) These two nearly identical phrases, by two of Christ's disciples, make it very difficult to argue that this was by mistake.

The third reason suggesting a mid-tribulation rapture is that placing the first half of Matthew 24:29 (the blood moons) in correct chronological order after Matthew 24:9 shows us the same skip over the first part of the Great Tribulation, before the rapture as in Revelation 6 between verses 12 and 13. The rapture is mentioned in Matthew 24:27, 28, 31, 40-41.

Read in this order, it occurs in chronological order as follows:

"Then they will deliver you to **tribulation**, and will kill you, and you will be hated by all nations on account of My name." (Matt. 24:9, NASB, EM). Matthew 24:29 "But immediately **after <u>the tribulation of those days</u>** THE SUN WIL BE DARKENED, AND THE MOON WILL NOT GIVE ITS LIGHT, …" (Matt.24:29 (NASB, EM).

Please note that when the first half of Matt. 24:29 - the blood moons, are placed after Matt. 24:9, the blood moons now occur immediately after the martyrdom of Matt. 24:9. This is the same order as it occurs in Rev. 6. Martyrdom occurs in Rev. 6:9-11 and then the blood moons occur in Rev. 6:12. This is important as it explains the timing of events and that all the events in Rev. chapter 6 and Matt. 24 occur in the same order. This is very improbable and lets us know that this was done intentionally. Since placing the first portion of Matt. 24:29 after Matt. 24:9 causes the blood moons to occur in the same order as in Rev. 6, it confirms that Christ's statement "immediately after the tribulation of those days," was intended to let us know that the blood moons are ordered after Matt. 24:9. There is a one page overview at the end of the third proof.

The blood moons spoken of are almost certainly the set that ran from 2014–2015. The following events start an uptick during or near the end the blood moons: "And **at that time** many will fall away and will deliver up one another and hate one another. 11 "And many false prophets will arise, and will mislead many. 12 **And because of lawlessness is increased, most people's love will grow cold.**" (Matt. 24:10-12, NASB, EM).

Has lawlessness recently taken an uptick? Riots, murders etc.?

"The sun will be turned into darkness, and the moon to into blood, **before the great and awesome day of the Lord comes.**" (Joel 2:31, NASB). That is the blood moons occur before the last portion of the Great Tribulation, the awesome wrath. This also almost certainly describes the same four blood moons previously mentioned.

Does the following verse remind you of any current events? "And because lawlessness is increased, most people's love will grow cold" (Matt. 24:12, NASB). In Ferguson and Baltimore, elected officials order police not to stop the rioting, illegal robbing and burning, some cities experiencing more break-ins, and terrorism. An elected official saying, "If you like your health care plan, you can keep it..." then the opposite happens? This is not a problem for just one political party, nor just for political parties but obvious examples of injustice occurring in society. (https://www.youtube.com/watch?v=qpa-5jdCnmo; 3/28/2016 www.politifact.com/truth-o-meter/article/2013/dec/12/lie-year-if-you-like-your-health-care-plan-keep-it/). 3/28/2016

Bernie Madoff and others committed white-collar theft. The Supreme Court, instead of judging what a written statement in a particular bill means, which is their job, say something such as, "We think this is what was intended." Therefore no law necessarily means what it says; it can mean almost anything. Lawlessness could also be without law, as people do whatever they wish, basically anarchy.

Then more importantly, there are God's laws being broken, which is the real lawlessness—the core point of the verse. Many of America's laws previously reflected God's law. Now that is changing.

True, these types of events have happened from time to time in the past. However it is a matter of intensity, as the passage says "And because lawlessness is <u>increased, **most people's love will grow cold."**</u> (NASB, EM). At this time, various types of lawlessness continue getting worse and worse—more riots, home invasions, people being beaten, used, and abused until eventually most people don't care what happens to others. You might want to follow the murder rate per year and see if it starts increasing with any significance from 2014 and 2015 on.

If the first half of Matthew 24:29, which is the first portion of what I am calling a "split verse," was intended to follow after Matthew 24:9, then the four blood moons, which started in 2014, should mark the start of increased lawlessness. Winter weather will deter some violence.

The Effect of Placing the Blood Moons in the Intended Order
Dan. 12:4 "… many shall run to and fro …" (KJV)

Aprox. 1914

The five seals—false Christs, war, famine, and martyrdom—all occur at the same time. They are separated here to give a feeling of the passage of time.

World War I

Matt. 24:4&5 False Christs	Rev. 6:2 The White Horse
Matt. 24:6 War	Rev. 6:3&4 The Red Horse

World War II

Matt. 24:32 The fig tree	1948 Israel is reborn	Isa. 66:8 Reborn in one day
Martyrdom escalates	A set of four blood moons	Rev. 6:11 No. of martyrs not complete
Matt. 24:7 Famines		Rev. 6:5&6 The Black Horse
The Six Day War 1967	Israel defends itself	Jerusalem is again Israel's
Another set of blood moons		No. of martyrs not complete
Matt. 24:8 Birth pangs	Suffering gets worse	Rev. 6:7&8 The Ashen Horse
Dan. 12:4	Approx. 1990	The Information Age
Matt. 24:9 Christians killed—"tribulation"		**Rev. 6:9-11** Martyrdom

More Christians killed for their faith in the past 60 yrs. than in all prior history. The unique set of four blood moons 2014–2015

Matt. 24:29 "...THE MOON WILL NOT GIVE ITS LIGHT" **Rev. 6:12** The blood moons following on Jesus's cue "But immediately after the <u>tribulation of those days</u>…" Matt. 24:29 (NASB). Placing the first half of Matt. 24:29 after Matt 24:9, the blood moons now come after Christians are killed (martyred) in Matt.24:9, just as in Rev. 6:9-11,12, as Christians are killed (martyred) and then immediately after come the blood moons. This confirms moving the first half of Matt. 24:29 to after Matt. 24:9 is correct. This seems to confirm where we are on the time line now.

Matt. 24:12	Lawlessness increases	
Matt. 24:15-21	The Great Tribulation begins	
Matt. 24:22-26	Christians endure more persecution and martyrdom	
Matt. 24:27-28, 30-31	The Rapture	Rev. 7:9-17

Matt. 24:29 "THE STARS WILL FALL" – God's wrath starts **Rev.6:13-17**

Please notice that in chapter 15, in "The Second Parallel View," the side-by-side comparison of Revelation 6 and Matthew 24 shows specific words in bold type. In Matthew 24:3, Jesus' disciples ask, "**When** will these things be?" (NASB, EM). This is a question about timing. In Matthew 24:4 through 24:8, Jesus talks about the five seals—false Christs, war, famine, birth pangs, and martyrdom. After this Jesus says "**then**" Christians will be martyred: "deliver you to tribulation." Jesus continues His dialogue in the order these events—"these things"—occur, showing us so by the use of the words "when," "beginning," "then," and "after."

The <u>FOURTH</u> proof of a mid-tribulation rapture is the use of the word "then," telling us the order of events.

Matthew 24:9 "**Then** they will deliver you to tribulation, and will kill you, and you will be hated by all nations on account of My name." (NASB, EM)

The 2014 and 2015 blood moons occur at this point in time.

In Matthew 24:14, Jesus talks about the gospel being preached to all nations, and "**then** *the end shall come.*" (NASB, EM). "The end," as is next explained in Matthew 24:15–22, is the Great Tribulation.

"Therefore **when** you <u>see</u> the ABOMINATION OF DESOLATION …" (Matt. 24:15, NASB, EM). This is the beginning of the end of the era, the start of the Great Tribulation.

"**then** let those who are in Juda flee to the mountains;" (Matt. 24:16, NASB, EM)

"for **then** there will be a <u>great tribulation</u>, such as had not occurred since the beginning of the world until now, nor ever shall." (Matt. 24:21, NASB, EM). This is the same Great Tribulation that has been referred to throughout this book. The Great Tribulation begins before God's wrath starts in Matthew 24:29.

The Antichrist, the abomination of desolation, desecrates the holy sanctuary. The Israelis—Jews—are told to flee, and Jesus says that "**then**" there will be a Great Tribulation. The desecration of the temple is the key to knowing the Great Tribulation is starting. The lawlessness was bad; now things get worse.

What happens next in time?

"**Then** if anyone says to you, 'Behold, here is the Christ,' or 'There He is,' do not believe him." (Matt. 24:23, NASB, EM). Jesus is now talking about Christians who might try to find Christ. Who would look for the Christ? Most Jews, who do not yet believe Jesus is the Messiah the Christ, are not likely to look for Christ. Atheists are not interested in looking for the risen Christ, as they don't think there is a Messiah. This means there are those who are setting traps, hunting down Christians to be martyred. Jesus is saying, "Don't go there; I, Jesus, am returning in the sky."

There is more evidence that Matthew 24:29 is a split verse, split by time. "*But immediately <u>after the tribulation of those </u>days THE SUN WILL BE DARKENED, AND THE MOON WILL NOT GIVE ITS LIGHT, …*" (NASB, EM) This likely comes years (approximately 7-14) before the last portion of the Great Tribulation, mentioned in the last portion of Matt. 24:29 The Great Tribulation has not started yet and the rapture did not occur at the time of the blood moons, or we missed it. There must be time between the two events.

Following in order "For just as the lightning comes from the east, and flashes even to the west, so shall the coming of the Son of Man be. 28 "Wherever the corpse is, there the vultures will gather." (Matt. 24:27-28, NASB) [Christ returns and angels are described finding Christians, this is the rapture.] "…**AND THE STARS WILL FALL FROM THE SKY**, …" (Matt. 24:29, NASB, EM). [This is God's wrath and occurs after the first part of the Great Tribulation. Now occurring very close in time, Christ's return, people complaining about God's wrath and then the rapture is mentioned again in Matt. 24:30&31.] "and **then** the sign of the Son of Man will appear in the sky, and **then** all the <u>tribes of the earth will mourn, and they will see the Son of </u>Man COMING ON THE CLOUDS OF THE SKY with power and great glory. 31 "And He will send forth His angels with A GREAT TRUMPET and THEY WILL GATHER TOGETHER HIS elect …" (Matt. 24:30&31 NASB, EM)

As seen previously, this is what is mentioned in Revelation 6:12: "…*and the sun became black as sackcloth made of hair, and the whole moon became like blood;*" (NASB, EM). [In order: the blood moons come after Matthew 24:9, before the Great Tribulation starts; then the Great Tribulation, then the rapture, then God's wrath in Revelation 6:13 occurs:] "**and the stars of the sky fell to the earth, as a fig tree cast its unripe figs when shaken by a great wind.**" (NASB, EM).

The three verses which follow, in Revelation 6:16–17, explain that this is God's "wrath." Obviously these two passages are talking about God's wrath in the form of stars—luminous objects, likely meteors, meteorites—as fire and brimstone falling to earth.

As Joel 2:31 mentions, the sun becomes dark and moon looks like blood <u>before</u> the awesome day of the Lord. Then years later the Great Tribulation and God's wrath occur here in Revelation 6:13 and Matthew 24:29.

Since the four blood moons occur over a two-year period, the two-year sequence could not occur moments before the stars fall from the sky and include time for the first half of the Great Tribulation to occur. Other wise the stars – fire and brimstone would have fallen during the blood moons and that did not occur.

Both Matthew 24:29 and Revelation 6:13 say "<u>and</u> **the stars of the sky fell**" (NASB, EM). If the word "and" were intended to mean that the blood moons and the stars falling from the sky happen at the same time, then meteors of God's wrath should have fallen in 2014 and 2015, killing many. In addition the stars falling are God's wrath and Christians are not subject to God's wrath. There has to be a split, a time period that occurs between the blood moons and the stars falling from the sky. This time period is likely approximately seven to fourteen years.

A different miraculous event would be about the only other thing that could fulfill this prophecy. However, the blood moons have accompanied significant biblical prophecy in the past, such as the rebirth of Israel—"have you ever seen a nation born in a day?" A set of blood moons occurred during that time.

The set of four blood moons that occurs in 2014–15 is the last set this century that occurs on Jewish High Holy Days. Therefore, this set of blood moons must be the set spoken of in Revelation 6:12, Matthew 24:29, and Joel 2:31.

The use of the word "then" in the previous verses explains the sequence of events. This was the fourth proof that it is a mid-tribulation rapture. The order of events place the rapture in the middle of the Great Tribulation.

All this confirms that Matthew 24:29 is split: the four blood moons come before the Great Tribulation, and the stars falling (God's wrath being poured out) occur at the end of the first portion of the Great Tribulation, that is in the middle of the Great Tribulation.

Some people might suggest that there is another rapture before the Great Tribulation. How so? Matthew 24:21; Mark 13:19; Luke 21:20, 23; Daniel 12:1 (another split verse); and Revelation 7:14 are about the only verses that make specific reference to the Great Tribulation. These all refer to the same verses we have been looking at. As the events in Matthew 24 and Revelation 6 have been ordered, Revelation 7:9-17 (of primary interest Rev. 7:14) is a leap from earth to heaven. It speaks of the rapture and comes in order right after Revelation 6:12–13. Perhaps immediately after—the rapture and wrath may come so close together, that they may be difficult to separate in time.

"**After** these things I looked, and behold, a great multitude, which no one could count, from every nation and all tribes and peoples and tongues, standing before the throne and before the Lamb, ..." (Rev. 7:9, NASB). This number of people who have been raptured is huge. There would not be a huge number of people to be raptured out of the last portion of the Great Tribulation, which is God's wrath, since these people have already been given great opportunity to repent and follow Christ and did not. Again, no previous rapture is mentioned.

Shown again in brief, the fourth proof that this is a mid-tribulation rapture is the way Jesus places the events in order, using the word "then." The next section, "Verse by Verse," will, I hope, make this easier to understand. Some of you will find this redundant and frustrating. However, it may be just what makes the concept understandable for others.

Verse - By - Verse The Sequential Order Abbreviated

Jesus in Matthew 24:6: "…but that is **not yet** the end." (NASB, EM).

Matthew 24:8: "…the **beginnings** of birth pangs." (NASB, EM).

Matthew 24:9: "**Then** they will deliver you to _tribulation_, and will kill you, and you will be hated by all nations on account of My name." (NASB, EM).

Matthew 24:29: "But immediately **after** the tribulation of **those** days THE SUN WILL BE DARKENED, AND THE MOON WILL NOT GIVE ITS LIGHT, …" (NASB, EM). Notice _tribulation_—the suffering—in this verse and Matthew 24:9, which "_those days_" must refer to.

Joel 2:31: "The sun will be turned into darkness, and the moon into blood, **before** the great and awesome day of the Lord comes." (NASB). These blood moons occurred from early 2014 through September 2015.

Matthew 24:12: "…lawlessness is increased, …" (NASB).

The temple in Jerusalem is rebuilt per Daniel 9:25–26.

Matthew 24:14: "And this gospel of the kingdom shall be preached in the whole world for a witness to all the nations, and **then the end shall come.**" (NASB, EM).

The sacrifices must be started, since Daniel 9:27 says they will be stopped. The sacrifices are to be carried out for three and a half years before Matthew 24:15 occurs.

Matthew 24:15: "Therefore **when** you see the ABOMINATION OF DESOLATION which was spoken of through Daniel the prophet, standing in the holy place …" (NASB, EM).

Matthew 24:16: "**then** let those who are in Judea flee to the mountains;" (NASB, EM).

Matthew 24:21: "for **then** there will be a Great Tribulation, …" (NASB, EM). This indicates the Great Tribulation started with the abomination of desolation in the Temple, verse 15.

Christians are persecuted, traps set, and Christians martyred.

Matthew 24:23: "**Then** if anyone says to you, 'Behold, here is the Christ,' or 'There He is,' do not believe him." (NASB, EM).

Matthew 24:28: "Wherever the corpse is, there the vultures will gather." (NASB). This is the rapture.

The rapture was mentioned in Matthew 24:27 "…the coming of the Son of Man…" (NASB) and Matthew 24:28 "Wherever the corpse is, there the vultures will gather." (NASB) Just as vultures find the dead, angels will find Christians and participate in the rapture. Revelation 7 is a jump from earth to heaven. In Revelation 7:1 angels are holding back the wind from blowing on earth. This will likely be eerie and many animals will likely run for a place to hide. The one hundred and forty-four thousand Jews are receiving a seal of protection as the wind is being held back. From Revelation 7:9 – 17 we are told of Christians who (Rev. 7:14) were raptured from the midst of the Great Tribulation. Revelation 8:1 mentions silence in heaven, which occurs for about half an hour, which seems to be the amount of time angels hold the wind from blowing and Christians are greeted into heaven. Revelation 8:5-11 is most likely talking about the same fire and brimstone as mentioned in Matthew 24:29 and Revelation 6:13-17, which is the beginning of the second portion of the Great Tribulation, God's wrath.

"And He will send forth His angles with A GREAT TRUMPET and THEY WILL GATHER TOGETHER HIS elect from the four winds, from one end of the sky to the other." Matt.24:31 (NASB). This is the rapture.

The rapture occurs, then very soon wrath.

Matthew 24:29: "...THE STARS WILL FALL FROM THE SKY, ..." (NASB). Fire and brimstone falling.

Matthew 24:30: "and **then** the sign of the Son of Man will appear in the sky, and **then** all the tribes of the earth will mourn, ..." (NASB, EM).

This tells us that Christians living today, who are alive when the Great Tribulation starts, will have to go through the first portion of the Great Tribulation.

The <u>FIFTH</u> evidence of a mid-tribulation rapture is Joel 2:31: "The sun will be turned into darkness, and the moon into blood, **before** the great and awesome day of the Lord comes." (NASB, EM). "The great and awesome day of the Lord" seems to refer to the last half of the Great Tribulation—God's powerful, awesome wrath. The blood moons occur, then the rapture, and then wrath; however, the rapture is mentioned before and after the blood moons.

Revelation 6:9-11 talks of martyrdom as does Matt. 24:9. Next in Revelation 6:12-13 come the topics of blood moons and stars falling from the sky, which does not occur in Matthew until Matt. 24:29. Therefore Rev. 6:12-13 has just skipped 20 verses in Matthew 24 which is a skip in time as it has skipped over events that occur. In Matthew 24:29 the blood moons and the stars falling from the sky also come back to back, yet it would seem that the same period of time, the same skip of time - events would occur between the first half of the verse, the blood moon and the stars falling from the sky. There is evidence for this.

If, if the phrase "...the tribulation of those days ..." (NASB) in Matthew 24:29 referred to the first part of the Great Tribulation, then the first part of the Great Tribulation would have to be over before the blood moons to have occurred from 2014-2015. The Great Tribulation has not started yet. This also rules out the blood moons occurring after the entire Great Tribulation, since Jesus used the word *"then"*, the last portion is ongoing in Matthew 24:30, as tribes mourn. If Matthew 24:9 were speaking of the Great Tribulation, then the rapture would come after the Great Tribulation since it is referred in Matt. 29 and Christians are not subject to God's wrath.

Again this means the blood moons from the first half of Matthew 24:29 must come in sequential order after Matthew 24:9, followed by the first half of the Great Tribulation, then the rapture, and then God's wrath. This implies a mid-tribulation rapture. In this way the blood moons of Matt. 24:29 come before "the great and awesome day of the Lord," as Joel 2:31 states.

Much of what has been discussed is that every subject in Revelation 6 comes in the same order as Matthew 24. However, when Matthew 24 and Revelation 6 are placed side by side, as in "The Second Parallel View" (see chapter 15), we see that Revelation 6 just skips over the first portion of the Great Tribulation. If we place the Great Tribulation in order with Matthew, the skip occurs in between Revelation 6:12 and Revelation 6:13. This implies there is a mid-tribulation rapture that simply is not mentioned in Revelation 6. Such a conclusion is also implied in the context of Revelation 6 and Revelation 7:14: "…These are the ones who come out of the great tribulation, …"(NASB).

The SIXTH reason, though perhaps redundant, is that Revelation 6:13 mentions stars falling and then wrath in Revelation 6:16–17, which happens just after the rapture in Matthew 24:27–28. This also explains that this is a mid-tribulation rapture. This is reliable since both Revelation 6 and Matthew 24 cover the same subjects in the same order. The rapture is simply mentioned again in Matt. 24:30-31.

Split Verses

There is some more context to these verses which are being called "split verses"—split by time (a sentence or two verses split by "and" in the original Greek and a semicolon or a comma in English), since an event such as the four blood moons occurs, then there is a time period of 1,335 days which pass, or in other verses seven to fourteen or even seventeen years pass, before the second event occurs, such as stars falling from the sky. The last days must cover about one hundred fourteen years, likely from approximately 1914 to 2028 or perhaps 2033. Seven to fourteen years is a short period of time compared to one hundred fourteen years, and very short time since the prophecies were first made. Whatever God's purpose, the seven to eleven years have been compressed between the first and second half of a sentence or two verses, split by "and" and addressing two separate events.

"And I looked when He broke the sixth seal, and there was a great earthquake; and the sun became black as sackcloth made of hair, and the whole moon became like blood;" (Rev. 6:12, NASB) [—the blood moons come before the Great Tribulation; "and" and the semicolon splits the verse, and approximately seven to fourteen years pass. Then the rapture occurs, and then wrath—] "13 and the stars of the sky fell to the earth," (Rev. 6:13, NASB).

Another split occurs in Matthew 24. "But immediately after the tribulation of those days THE SUN WILL BE DARKEND, AND THE MOON WILL NOT GIVE ITS LIGHT," (verse 29)[—here it splits and seven to fourteen years go by; then-]"**and** the stars will fall from the sky, and the powers of the heavens will be shaken 30 and then the sign of the Son of Man will appear in the sky, ..." (verses 29–30, NASB, EM). Again "and" and a comma (in translation) have been used to make the split, as it has been translated into English. The first half of Matthew 24:29 is talking about blood moons soon before the Great Tribulation. The first portion of Matt. 24:29 – the blood moons – occur in time after the suffering – the "tribulation" (not the Great Tribulation) – mentioned in Matt. 24:9. The second portion - event, occurs in time 20 verses later. This skip to the second event – "the stars falling from the sky – seems to occur 7 – 14 years later. The rapture occurs in Matt. 24:27&28, then God's wrath, the stars falling from the sky. The verse skips in time, splitting the first subject – event, from the second event, by approximately 7 – 14 years. Why? Perhaps God did not want the mid-tribulation clearly revealed to all until a later time.

There is a very similar split in Mark 13:24–25. "But in those days, after **that** tribulation, THE SUN WILL BE DARKENED, AND THE MOON WILL NOT GIVE ITS LIGHT," (verse 24) [—approximately seven to fourteen years pass —] 25 "AND THE STARS WILL BE FALLING from heaven, and the powers that are in the heavens will be shaken." (NASB, EM). Again, a comma and "and" are the only things that seem to separate the time that passes. There is nothing in Mark chapter 13, to prove there is a passage of time between verses twenty-four and twenty-five. The evidence that they are a split verse is that they refer to the same events and context as Matthew chapter 24 and the comparison to Revelation chapter six.

What would suggest a time period of approximately 7 to 14 years pass between the blood moons and the stars falling from the sky? Jesus mentioned the things which would take place before the mentioned generation expired. If we use seventy years from Psalm 90:10 as the end of the generation Jesus mentioned, there is not enough time for everything Jesus mentioned to occur. Adding the eighty years found in Psalm 9:10 as the time span of a generation and adding that to Israel's date of rebirth—1948, gives approximately 2028. The blood moons started in 2014 giving fourteen years until 2028 for the things Christ mentioned to take place. In Matt. 24:34 Jesus says all <u>these</u> things will take place before this generation expires and Matt. 24:15-27 does describe the first portion of the Great Tribulation. Before the Great Tribulation starts The Temple must be rebuilt, a treaty signed and three and a half years of sacrifices carried out which all might require about seven years. Based on these things approximately 7 to 14 years must take place from 2014, the blood moons, until the end of the first portion of the Great Tribulation is over and God starts delivering wrath on the earth in the form of stars falling from the sky.

A <u>SEVENTH</u> evidence of a mid-tribulation rapture. Again a similar split occurs in the second sentence of Daniel 12:1. "Now at that time Michael, the great prince who stands guard over the sons of your people, will arise. And there will be a **time of distress** such as never occurred since there was a nation until that time**;**"[—there is a split and 1,335 days (?) go by—]"… **and** at that time your people, everyone who is found written in the book, will be **rescued**. 2 "And many of those who sleep in the dust of the ground will awake, these to everlasting life, but the others to disgrace and everlasting contempt." (NASB, EM). The time of distress is the first part of the Great Tribulation. The Great Tribulation starts, then approximately three and a half years later Christians are "rescued," which is the rapture.

Again, "and" and a semicolon in English, make the split. People are saved from the last half of the Great Tribulation, God's wrath, implying a mid-tribulation rapture.

A "time of distress such as never occurred since there was a nation until that time;" (NASB). [This is the Great Tribulation almost exactly as Christ stated it in Matthew] 24:21: "for then there will be a great tribulation, such as has not occurred since the beginning of the world until now, nor ever shall." (NASB).

Is this perspective conjecture or simply a wild guess? There are more specific verses suggested in Daniel to support the mid-tribulation view.

The <u>EIGHTH</u> indicator of a mid-tribulation rapture is found in Daniel 11:31: "And forces from him will arise, desecrate the sanctuary fortress, and do away with the regular sacrifice. And they will set up the **abomination of desolation.**" (NASB, EM). This verse starts a passage that follows the same time line and describes the same circumstances found in Matthew 24:15–26, which is the first half of the Great Tribulation.

"Therefore when you see the ABOMINATION OF DESOLATION which was spoken of through Daniel the prophet, standing in the holy place (let the reader understand)" (Matt. 24:15, NASB). The two passages both start off talking about the "abomination of desolation" in the Temple. The passages that follow in both Daniel and Matthew then give glimpses of what Christians will endure during the first part of the Great Tribulation.

"And by smooth words he will turn to godlessness those who act wickedly toward the covenant, but the people who know their God will display strength and take action. 33 "And those who have insight among the people will give understanding to the many; yet they will fall by sword and by flame, by captivity and by plunder, for many days. 34 "Now when they fall they will be granted a little help, and many will join with them in hypocrisy. 35 "And some of those who have insight will fall, in order to refine, purge, and make them pure, until the <u>end time</u>; because it is still to come at the appointed time." (Dan. 11:32-34, NASB, EM).

Here in Daniel 11:35 the "end time" appears to refer specifically to the last part of the Great Tribulation.

"Then if anyone says to you, "Behold, here is the Christ,' or 'There He is,' do not believe him. 24 "For false Christs and false prophets will arise and will show great signs and wonders, so as to mislead, if possible, even the elect. 25 "Behold, I have told you in advance. 26 "If therefore they say to you, 'Behold, He is in the wilderness,' do go forth, or 'Behold, He is in the inner rooms,' do not believe them. 27 "For just as the lightning come from the east, and flashes even to the west, so shall the coming of the Son of Man be. 28 "Wherever the corpse is, there the vultures will gather." [This is the rapture.] 29 "But immediately after the tribulation of **those** days THE SUN WILL BE DARKENED, AND THE MOON WILL NOT GIVE ITS LIGHT, [now wrath starts] AND THE STARS WILL FALL from the sky, and the powers of the heavens will be shaken." (Matt. 24:23-29, NASB, EM).

Wrath is not mentioned in Daniel 11:32–35 nor Matthew 24:15–27, as it starts in the second half of Matthew 24:29.

A NINETH possible indicator of a mid-tribulation rapture is found in Isaiah. "Come, my people, enter into your rooms, and close your doors behind you; hide for a little while, until indignation runs its course. 21 For behold, the Lord is about to come out from His place to punish the inhabitants of the earth for their iniquity; ...27:1 In that day the Lord will punish Leviathan the fleeing serpent, …" (Isa. 26:20-21,27:1, NASB, EM). The phrase "my people," is almost certainly God talking to His people—Christians and Messianic Jews (Jewish Christians) who are told to hide from "indignation." Christians are not appointed to God's wrath. Therefore these Christians are being told to hide from the furious anger of the abomination of desolation or indirectly, Leviathan the fleeing serpent... the dragon and the events he has instigated. Then in verse 21 God pours out wrath after the rapture. This passage is almost certainly talking about the first half of the Great Tribulation, just as Matthew 24:15–26 and Daniel 11:32–35.

Now, out of written sequence, the rapture is described:

"Your dead <u>will live;</u> their corpses <u>will rise. You who lie in the dust, awake</u> and shout for joy, for your dew is as the dew of the dawn, and the earth will give birth to departed spirits." (Isa. 26:19, NASB, EM). [The rapture]

"...and you will be gathered up one by one, O sons of Israel. 13 It will come about also in that day that a great trumpet will be blown; ..." (Isa. 27:12–13, NASB). [The rapture]

We can be fairly confident that this passage, which speaks about the rising of the dead, is the rapture. Three times the passage says "will"—it is going to happen, yet the passage does not say "now." Although this means Isaiah 26:19 does not necessarily happen in the order it is written, it is most likely similar to Matthew 24:27-31 when the rapture is mentioned, then the blood moons, then wrath and the rapture is mentioned again. Isaiah 27:12–13 also mention the rapture, which comes with a trumpet blast twelve verses later.

The last part of the Great Tribulation is God's wrath. "For behold, the Lord is about to come out from His place to punish the inhabitants of the earth for their iniquity; and the earth will reveal her bloodshed, and will no longer cover her slain." (Isa. 26:21, NASB). The rapture has just occurred or is occurring; then God's wrath is poured out on those who did not repent. The passage says that God will "come out from His place," just as Isaiah 64:1 mentions the heavens—the sky being rent, ripped open like a curtain, revealing Christ.

"In that day the Lord will punish Leviathan the fleeing <u>serpent,</u> with His fierce and great and mighty sword. Even Leviathan the twisted serpent; and He will kill the dragon who lives in the sea." (Isa. 27:1, NASB, EM). Genesis 3:1 talks about the "serpent" in the garden—Satan. Revelation 20:2, 14 talks of Satan being thrown in the lake of fire, called the second death. Isaiah 27:1 talks about the Lord Christ, killing Satan, as in throwing him in to the lake of fire, the second death, eternal torment.

This explanation may not be satisfying for some of you. This idea places Isaiah 26:20 as the first half of the Great Tribulation. Isaiah 26:19 shows the rapture. In this way not all of the events occur in written order. If the order of events were Isaiah 26:19 (the rapture) first, then why would there be Christians on earth who were told to "hide"? Who would be "my people" on earth just after the rapture? Only the 144,00 Jews remain. Who would have evangelized them so quickly?

The events in Isaiah chapters 26 and 27 almost certainly indicate a mid-Great Tribulation rapture.

The view that the first half of Matthew 24:29—"But immediately after the tribulation of those days THE SUN WILL BE DARKENED, AND THE MOON WILL NOT GIVE ITS LIGHT, ..."— (NASB), should come after Matthew 24:9—" ...deliver you to tribulation ..." (NASB)—occur in this order may be a point of confusion.

When Matthew 24:29 says "...**after** the tribulation of those days ..."(NASB, EM), the word "after" might lead us to think that the "tribulation" of those days, the martyrdom, is now over. However, in Matthew 24:23–26, we can clearly see that Christians are still being hunted down and killed for their belief. This sounds like a contradiction. You can have confidence there is no contradiction. Something else has happened. The circumstances are just the same as in the first two chapters in Job, Satan has received permission to continue his rage.

In Job 1, Satan came before God and received permission to cause Job suffering by the loss of his family and some friends. Job did not fail the test, and Satan was not satisfied with the results. Satan received a second opportunity to further cause Job pain. Comparing the first five seals of Revelation 6 with Job 1 and 2, it becomes almost certain that Satan did not accomplish his goals in Matthew 24:4–9/Revelation 6:1–11, in the wars, famines, pestilence, and martyrdom occurring from 1914 through 2014. Just as he did in Job 2, it appears Satan has asked to martyr more Christians and cause more war, more famine, more pestilence, more earthquakes, more lawlessness, and more hate. There is no statement in Matthew 24 or

Revelation 6 to absolutely confirm that Satan has asked for and received permission to continue or expand his terror, aside from perhaps the birth pangs, the ashen horse. However, it is likely, since it follows the pattern set in Job and the first five seals in Revelation 6.

A <u>TENTH</u> possible indicator for a mid-tribulation rapture is found in Daniel 12: "Many will be purged, purified and refined; ..." Dan. 12:10 (NASB) [these being purified are Christians in the first part of the Great Tribulation, as in Daniel 11:35] "...but the wicked will act wickedly, and none of the wicked will understand, but those who have insight will understand." Dan.12:10 [Those who understand are Christians in the first part of the Great Tribulation.] 11 "And from the time that the regular sacrifice is abolished, and the abomination of desolation is set up, there will be 1,290 days. 12 "How blessed is he who keeps waiting and attains to the 1,335 days!" (Daniel 12:10-12, NASB).

The passage mentions "attains" – Christians who have not died or do not deny Christ for the 1,335 days, which is almost certainly the first part of the Great Tribulation, implying a mid-tribulation rapture.

Many of us were taught or unconsciously came to the conclusion that the entire seven years of the Great Tribulation represent God's wrath. Those of us who thought this and those who taught this were almost certainly wrong.

The first half of the Great Tribulation is Satan's wrath. The trigger to the Great Tribulation starts in Matthew 24:15 with the abomination of desolation in the place he should not be. In Matthew 24:21, we see the start of the Great Tribulation stated by Jesus. Then we see Satan most likely indirectly inflicting suffering and killing Christians in Matthew 24:22–27.

Then the rapture occurs. Then in the second part of Matthew 24:29, God starts pouring out His wrath. Those who have not committed their lives to Christ will suffer during the entire Great Tribulation. However, they do not appear to be the primary target of Satan's wrath in the first half.

It might be worthwhile to search the Bible and see if you can find any passage that states clearly says or implies that the entire seven years of the Great Tribulation is the wrath of God. The concept of seven years of God's wrath seems to be a subconscious assumption, not based on evidence.

Three Reasons in Brief or Perhaps Twelve

1. "And one of the elders answered, saying to me," "These who are clothed in the white robes, who are they, and from where have they come?" 14 And I said to him, "My lord, you know," And he said to me, "These are the ones **who come out of the great tribulation**, and they have washed their robes and made them white in the blood of the Lamb." (Rev. 7:13-14, NASB, EM). The phrase "out of" in the original Greek, means out of the middle of or out of the midst of, not before and not after. This is a mid-Great Tribulation rapture.

2. Comparing Revelation 6 to Matthew 24, we can see that Revelation 6 skips over Matthew 24:10–28. The events Revelation 6 skips over in Matthew 24 come just before the abomination of desolation is set up, starting the Great Tribulation and the suffering Christians endure during the first portion. The rapture is then first mentioned in Matt. 24:27 &28. Revelation 6 then picks up just as God pours out his wrath at the beginning of the last half of the Great Tribulation in Matthew 24:29, these implying a mid-Great Tribulation rapture.

3. After noticing that Revelation skips over the Great Tribulation and placing Matthew 24:29 (the blood moons) after Matthew 24:9, it can be seen that Matthew 24 is following the same pattern as the skip in Revelation 6:12-13. This a mid–Great Tribulation rapture.

4. In Matthew 24, the word "then" is used to explain the order in which things occur. The only significant deviation from this order is by the use of the word "after" and the phrase "those days," referring to after Matthew 24:9. In order: the abomination of desolation is set up, starting the Great Tribulation; we see Christians suffering; the rapture occurs; and then God pour out His wrath.

5. "The sun will be turned into darkness, and moon into blood, **before** the great and awesome day of the Lord comes." (Joel 2:31, NASB). Joel clearly states the moon turns to blood before God's wrath and the unique blood moons occurred from 2014-2015, must be what Joel spoke of. These blood moons occurred before a new age has occurred and near the end of the generational time Jesus seems to have meant. The blood moons come after Matthew 24:9, which is before the Great Tribulation starts. The awesome day of the Lord refers to the last part of the Great Tribulation, when God's wrath is poured out. Christians are not appointed to wrath. Therefore the rapture has to occur before the wrath. There is no mention of the rapture until after the abomination of desolation is set up and Christians suffer.

6. In Luke 17:28–30, Jesus tells us that it will be just as it was in the days of Noah and Lot. In verse 30, Jesus says the day He is revealed will be like the day Lot fled Sodom to Zoar, and fire and brimstone fell. Lot was saved just before fire and brimstone, the stars fell from the sky and destroyed Sodom by God's wrath. So it will be just before God's wrath that comes after the first part of the Great Tribulation in Matthew 24. In Revelation 6:13–17, we are told of God's wrath raining down as stars, which means the rapture, God's saving of Christians, occurred earlier. This agrees with the statement in Revelation 7:14 speaking of those who came out of the Great Tribulation. In Genesis chapters 6&7 Noah and family enter the ark just before the flood, God's wrath. This is a mid-Great Tribulation rapture.

7. Revelation 8:1 starts with the seventh seal, a new, different event which is God's wrath, the first moments of which are mentioned in Revelation 6:13–17. In Revelation 7, we see what was occurring in heaven during the first minutes or hours after the wrath started. Revelation 8:1 picks up on the wrath. Since wrath is now being discussed and Christians are not appointed to wrath, and Rev.7:9 mentions "a great multitude" which "come out of the great tribulation" (NASB), the first part of the Great Tribulation must have already occurred. Again a mid-tribulation rapture.

8. " …And there will be **a time of distress such as never occurred since there was a nation** until that time; …"(Dan. 12:1, NASB, EM). [The phrase "never occurred" lets us know this suffering is a unique event.] "…; and at that time your people, everyone who is found written in the book, will be rescued." (Dan. 12:1, NASB). Christians have just been rescued from what? From God's wrath in the last part of the Great Tribulation. A pattern seems to have been set that in some cases, "and" is used in verses regarding the Great Tribulation, which separates events in time. The pattern includes a passage of time that encompasses the first part of the Great Tribulation. This seems to confirm that the rescue is from the last part of the Great Tribulation. Christians suffer during the first half of the Great Tribulation, the rapture occurs, and then wrath.

9. Daniel 11:31–32 starts with the abomination of desolation being set up. Then just as in Matthew 24:15–27, Christians are persecuted by the Antichrist, the abomination of desolation. As a reminder, the concept is that the first part of the Great Tribulation is Satan's wrath and the second half is God's wrath. Therefore, these Christians suffer Satan's wrath in Daniel 11:11–37 and will then be saved from God's wrath, the second portion. The same pattern is mentioned in Daniel 7:25–27. Satan, the abomination of desolation, speaks against God. He wears down the saints of God for time, times, and half a time, which seems to be the 1,335 days in Daniel 12:12. Out of apparent order, in Daniel 7:27, the saints will govern after the Great Tribulation is over, implying they were saved or raptured. Out of written order in Daniel 7:26, Satan is destroyed, which we know happens at the end of the last half of the Great Tribulation in Revelation 20. The same pattern again shows a mid-tribulation rapture.

10. "Many will be purged, purified and refined; but the wicked will act wickedly, and none of the wicked will understand, but those who have insight will understand. 11 "And from the time that the regular sacrifice is abolished, and the abomination of desolation is set up, there will be 1,290 days. 12 "How blessed is he who keeps waiting and attains to the 1,335 days!" (Daniel 12:10-12, NASB). Though not mentioned, the Temple in Jerusalem has already been rebuilt at this

time. Then the abomination of desolation is first set up as in Daniel 11:31 and Matthew 24:15. Then those being purified are Christians living during the first half of the Great Tribulation. This is seen in Daniel 11:32-36 and Matthew 24:23-26. The 1,335 days seems to be the amount of time the first part of the Great Tribulation lasts until the rapture occurs and Christians are saved from God's wrath.

11. In the passage of Isaiah 26:19–Isaiah 27:13. Isaiah 26:20 talks about God's people, who are told to hide. This implies that this happens during the first half or part of the Great Tribulation. Isaiah 27:12 says that His people will be gathered up, which is the rapture. Isaiah 27:13 says that there will be a great trumpet, and those who are approaching death will be saved, raptured, and worship the Lord. They are saved from the punishment of the wrath to come in Isaiah 26:21 & 27:7. Isaiah 26:21 talks about God – Christ who is revealed at the sound of the trumpet 27:13. Isaiah 26:19 speaks of those who have already died rising from the grave, again the rapture. Isaiah 27:1 talks about the slaying of Satan. This must be the least satisfying reason as there are no words which clearly indicate the chronological order. In addition the order of the events might not seem to indicate a mid-Great Tribulation order. On the other hand the rapture is clearly mentioned and God's people are told to hide. God's people almost certainly hiding from the wrath of the abomination of desolation and his henchmen.

In 1 Thessalonians 4:16–17 is the statement that those Christians who have already died will be raptured first, those in Isaiah 26:19. Christians who are alive then will be raptured (Isaiah 27:13). The time between the dead in Christ being raptured and those who are alive being raptured may be 30 minutes or a split second. The amount of time between the rapture and wrath will most likely be similar to the way Lot and Noah were saved from wrath on the same day wrath came.

12. 2 Thessalonians 2:1 starts by stating the topic. "…with regard to the **coming** of our Lord Jesus Christ, and our **gathering** together to Him.".… 3 "Let no one in any way deceive you, for it [Christ's return and our "gathering together"—the rapture] *will not come* unless.…

the **man of lawlessness is revealed**, the son of destruction 4 who opposes and exalts himself above every so-called god or object of worship, so that **he takes his seat in the temple of God, displaying himself as being God."** (2 Thess. 2:1,3&4, NASB) The initial topic is Christ's return and the Rapture. The verses that follow describe the very thing Jesus mentioned in Matt. 24:15, the abomination of desolation is seen, seen by whom? Christians are being spoken to. The abomination of desolation is seen by Christians and the first part of the Great Tribulation starts.

6 …"you know what restrains him… ["him" –God, who restrains the man of lawlessness] 9 that is, the one whose coming is in accord with the activity of Satan, with all power and signs and false wonders,… 3:3 But the Lord is faithful, and He will strengthen and protect you from the evil *one*." (2 Thessalonians 2: 6, 9, 3:3, NASB, EM). 2 Thess. chapter two is following the same pattern as Matt. 24, the abomination of desolation is seen, the Great Tribulation starts, then Christians suffer while God restrains Satan from even greater evil. The primary thing God seems to be doing when restraining is protecting Christians from losing their faith. Then.

"While **they** are saying, "Peace and safety!" then **destruction** will come upon **them** suddenly like **birth pangs** upon a woman with child: and **they** shall not escape… 9 For God has **not destined us for wrath**, but for obtaining salvation through our Lord Jesus Christ," (I Thessalonians 5:3&9, NASB, EM). 1 Thess. 5:3&9 tells us that "destruction", God's wrath comes "upon them," non-believers, while Christians do not suffer God's wrath, since Christians have just been raptured. This passage describes the same mid Great Tribulation rapture as Matt. 24. 1 Thess. 1:3&4 mentions that this day of destruction should not take Christians by surprise. We may not know the day or hour, however Christians should know that day is soon to come.

The book cover mentions three reasons to know whether it will be a pre-, post-, or mid-tribulation rapture. Twelve have been given, hoping you will find at least three you can agree with.

A One Page Overview of the End Times

Daniel 12:4 "…many shall run to and fro, …" (KJV)   Approx. 1914

False Christs, wars, famines, things get worse & martyrdom all occur at the same time. They are separated to give a sense of the passage of time.

Matt. 24:4&5 false Christs   Rev.6:1&2 The White Horse

Matt. 24:6 War   World War I   Rev. 6:3&4 The Red Horse

Matt. 24:32 The fig tree   Israel reborn 1948   Isa.66:8 In one day
A set of blood moons   Rev. 6:11 The number not complete

Matt.24:7 Famines   Rev. 6:5&6 The Black Horse

Dan. 12:4 "… and knowledge will increase." (NASB)   The Information Age

Matt. 24:8 Birth pangs   Rev. 6:7&8 The Ashen Horse

    The 9/11 Terrorist attack occurs   God is removing His protection

Matt. 24:9 Christians killed   "tribulation"   Rev. 6:9–11 Martyrdom

Matt.24:29 "… immediately after the tribulation of those days …" (NASB)

Matt. 24:29 The blood moons   2014–2015   Rev. 6:12 The blood moons

Now Matt.24:10–14 deliver one another up, false prophets, lawlessness, we must endure, Gospel preached. 14 "…then the end shall come."(NASB)

The Temple has been rebuilt   Dan.9:27 Israel signs 7 yr. peace treaty
    The sacrifices are started and are carried out for about 3½ years

Matt. 24:15 Abomination of Desolation   Dan. 11:31 The Abomination

Matt. 24:15–22   The Great Tribulation Starts   Dan. 12:1 Distress

Matt. 24:22–26   Christians suffer   Dan. 11:32–39 & 12:10–12

Matt. 24:27–28, 30–31   The Rapture   Dan. 12:1–2 Life rescued

Matt. 24:29 Stars fall   God's wrath   Rev. 6:13–17 & chaps.8–18

Matt. 24:30 Tribes mourn   Rev.6:15:-17 Tribes mourn

Rev. 20:4–6   Christ's thousand-year reign

17   Return to the Four Blood Moons

It is very important not to delude ourselves and therefore important to know if the series of blood moons we are talking about are actually unusual. From 1400 thru 2100 there are a total approaching 2,000 blood moons, which makes it possible that there are numerous tetrads– sets of four blood moons–during Nisan and Sukkot. An effort was made to find a list of Jewish High Holy days to compare to the Lunar Eclipses during the same time. The effort was not successful. However Wikipedia has provided a view that does not have a positive bias to this type of spiritual view. That is just what is needed.

"Writing for Earth & Sky Bruce McClure and Deborah Byrd point out that the reference verse also says the "sun will be turned into darkness," an apparent reference to a solar eclipse. They note that since the Jewish calendar is lunar, one sixth of all eclipses will occur during Passover or Sukkot. Furthermore, there have been 62 tetrads since the first century AD, though only eight of them have coincided with both feasts. Thus, the event is not as unusual as Hagee and Blitz imply. Additionally, three of the four eclipses in the tetrad were not even visible in the Biblical home land of Israel, casting further doubt on Hagee and Blitz's interpretation, even then, only the very end of the last eclipse was visible in Israel." https://en.wikipedia.org/wiki/Blood_moon_prophecy 5/15/2016

McClure and Byrd first point out the mention of solar eclipse in the quoted Bible verse. John Hagee did bring attention to the solar eclipses that accompanied the blood moons spoken of and Mark Blitz likely did the same. Why Byrd and McClure pointed this out is unknown. McClure and Byrd mention the 62 tetrads – groups of four blood moons in approximately 1,900 years. Then McClure and Byrd point out that of the 62 tetrads, only 8 occurred during both Passover – Nisan and Sukkot in approximately 2,000 years. That seems to be the very point that John Hagee and Blitz have made. Out of a ball park of 1,900 blood moons from 1400 to 2015, only four tetrads have occurred during these specific Jewish

High Holy days, and they were accompanied by historical important events affecting Jews.

On the contrary, using these specific criteria Hagee and or Blitz mention (blood moon tetrad, Nisan & Sukkot and very important Jewish historical events at the same time) it is very unusual, 4 for 4 in approximately 600 years of blood moons. I think you will find that Pastor Hagee mentions that it is unknown what important Biblical events may have occurred during some or all of the first four tetrads mentioned in earlier years. The further back in history we go, the more often we may not know of historic events. There is no point in arguing about the completely unknown.

In 1492, 1948, and 1967, these tetrads were accompanied by very historic events for Jews. In regard to the 2014 -2015 tetrad set, Joel stated the moon's eclipse – becoming a blood moon, would occur "before" Christ delivers vengeance – the event on those who reject Him. That event of wrath is yet to come. Three blood moon events, each one during the same Jewish High Holy days and each one, the only ones, accompanied by important historic Jewish events in approximately 600 years.

Byrd and McClure go on to discount the importance of these tetrads since "Additionally, three of the four eclipse in the tetrad were not even visible in the Biblical home land of Israel, …" The Mayan civilization had amazing calendar calculations and almost certainly knew some solar eclipse would be seen at locations on earth other than their location. The Magi knew astronomy well enough to calculate they needed to travel to Bethlehem. Astronomy today also tells us that these tetrads would occur even if not seen in our area. It is possible that God intended the tetrads as a warning for nations to repent. That most were not seen in Israel in no way means that these blood moons are not unusual as it was and is known that they occurred. Wikipedia's information was quite helpful.

There are points that we need to cover, for which credit is due to Pastor John Hagee. Pastor Hagee explains in his teaching that these are uncommon blood moons, as some or all occur Jewish High Holy days. These occurred —in 1492, 1948, and 1967— during Passover, Sukkoth, Nisan, and Adar.

Further, during these earlier sets, something bad happened and something good came out of it. In the 2014–2015 set all blood moons occur during Passover and Sukkoth.

The fourth set of four blood moons and solar eclipses started on April 15, 2014, and ended on September 28, 2015. This set of blood moons occurred on the Jewish High Holy Days. Three sets of four blood moons—the 1948 set, the 1967 set, and the 2014–2015 set—all three sets accompanied by Jewish High Holy Days, and all three sets occurring during the time period mentioned by Daniel and Jesus. The possibility of coincidence is improbable. It leads to another question.

As Joel 2:31 states, "The sun will be turned into darkness, and the moon into blood, **before** *the great and awesome day of the Lord comes.*" (NASB, EM). Three sets of blood moons occur during the time period Christ mentions and before the Great Tribulation starts. Which of the three sets of blood moon is referred to in Joel 2:31, Matthew 24:29, and Revelation 6:12?

Though it may not be obvious, the answer seems to be in a passage we have been reading. In Daniel 12:4, it seems clear that Daniel is talking about the latter part of the Industrial Age and the Information Age as the "end of time"—the end of a time period. Jesus speaks of the generational life span of those born in 1948, which would last through approximately 2028.

The generation living in 1492 lived long before the Industrial Age, and Israel had not been reborn, making it highly unlikely that this was the set of four blood moons being spoken of. The Information Age had not yet started at this time, and this generation was not passing away as Jesus mentioned in Matthew 24:34. Therefore, it is also unlikely that the blood moons that occurred in 1948 would be the set of blood moons spoken of in Joel 2:31, as this generation had just been born.

During the 1967 set of four blood moons, those born in 1948 would have been roughly nineteen years old. This does not come close to the seventy or eighty years mentioned in Psalm 90:10 for this generation to be coming close to passing away.

At this point the sets of four blood moons that began in the spring of 2014 -2015 would seem most likely to be the set spoken of in Joel 2:31. Is there anything else that would support this theory? Yes.

There is a clue in Revelation 6:12 "…and the sun became black as sackcloth *made* of hair, and **the whole moon became like blood**; …" (NASB, EM). This is talking about a "whole," a "total" lunar eclipse, not a partial lunar eclipse, nor near-total lunar eclipse.

The following list shows partial lunar eclipses, penumbral lunar eclipses (not quite total), and total lunar eclipses. Lunar eclipses before and after 1948 and 1967 are listed to allow you to see if any could be like the 2014–2015 set.

It is important to understand that a total eclipse of the sun or moon was only be seen to be total at certain locations on the earth.

This data on solar and lunar eclipses has been taken from Wikipedia.

1949	Oct 10	partial lunar eclipse	Oct 21	partial solar eclipse
1949	Apr 17	partial lunar eclipse	Apr 28	partial solar eclipse
1948	Sep 29	penumbral lunar	Nov 1	total solar eclipse
1948	Aug 30	penumbral lunar	May 9	annular solar eclipse
1948	Apr 5	penumbral lunar	May	annular solar eclipse
1948	Mar 6	penumbral lunar	Nov	annular solar eclipse
1947	Aug 20	partial lunar eclipse	Nov 12	annular solar eclipse
1947	Feb 13	total lunar eclipse	May 20	total solar eclipse

Lunar eclipses adjacent to 1948 and 1967 are also shown so that you can see for sure that they could not fulfill the prophecy of being "the whole moon," that is, total lunar eclipses. The Bible passages do not say that the solar eclipses need to be total.

1969	Apr 27	partial lunar eclipse	Mar 18	annular solar eclipse
1969	Oct 21	partial lunar eclipse	Sep 11	annular solar eclipse
1968	Oct 9	total lunar eclipse	Sep 22	total solar eclipse

1968	Apr 16	total lunar eclipse	Mar 22	partial solar eclipse
1967	**Apr 5**	**partial lunar eclipse**	**Nov 2**	**total solar eclipse**
1967	Sep 29	partial lunar eclipse	May 9	partial solar eclipse
1966	Feb 4	penumbral lunar eclp	May 20	annular solar eclipse
1966	Aug 20	penumbral lunar eclp	Nov 12	total solar eclipse

So far, all the blood moons that have occurred during the time Jesus and Daniel prophesied have missed fulfilling one factor—that the "whole" moon would turn to blood, i.e., total lunar eclipses.

2014	Apr 15	total lunar eclipse	Apr 29	annular solar eclipse
2014	Oct 8	total lunar eclipse	Oct 23	partial solar eclipse
2015	Apr 4	total lunar eclipse	Mar 20	total solar eclipse
2015	Sep 28	total lunar eclipse	Sep 13	partial solar eclipse

From 2014–2015, there were four total lunar eclipses. This was the last set this century that can fulfill the statements, in the time period Daniel mentioned and the time period Jesus mentioned and during a *shemitah*. All blood moons and solar eclipses occurred during Jewish High Holy Days and the last blood moon was a super moon, a harvest moon. Time is running out in the generational time period Jesus set. There does not seem to be much time left for it to start.

The 2014–2015 blood moon series seems to match what is required in Revelation 6:12: "the whole moon became like blood" (NASB). In Matthew 24:3, Christ's disciples ask for a "sign." Jesus says in Matthew 24:33, "even so you too, <u>when you see</u> **all** these things, *recognize that* **He is near, right at the door.**" (NASB, EM). The 2014-2015 blood moons are likely that sign, unless Christ's return is the sign.

Will it happen in a very similar manner to Christ's first arrival? In Matthew 2:1-2, we are told that the magi—wise men—saw Christ's brilliant star in the sky, light coming into the world. Then in Matthew 12:29 the scribes and Pharisees seemed to demand proof, a miraculous divine sign that only God could do, from Christ, which would prove that He was who He said He was, the Son of God. Christ said no sign would be given except for the sign of Noah, that is, that Jesus would rise from death in the grave on the third day, as He did and was taken up into the sky in Acts 1:9-11. Jesus did not pause nor cow to the Pharisees; the resurrection and ascension were already part of a predetermined plan.

Just as the star of Bethlehem was seen some time earlier than Christ's birth, so are the blood moons are almost certainly an early sign of Christ's return. The blood moons are not a never seen before miraculous event, yet are likely the prophesied unique solar and lunar eclipses, beautiful yet a foreboding darkening, signaling wrath in years soon to come. Then similar to Christ's mention of the sign of Noah and being seen leaving in the sky, the disciples ask for a sign, and in Matthew 24:30 it mentions "… the sign of the Son of Man will appear in the sky, …" (NASB), that is, Christ being seen coming in the sky as He left. The blood moons are a sign that John the Baptist and Christ's disciples would likely accept. The Pharisees would not ask for a unique set of blood moons as a sign, seen years before Christ's miraculously return, being seen returning in the sky. But, Christ returning in the sky, a miraculous sign, is the kind of miracle the Pharisees would want or demand before His coming, not a unique set of blood moons.

Christ did numerous amazing things during His stay on earth and many people believed due to those miracles. Now we believe for example, by hearing how Christ lived a life based on such an incredibly high standard of love. Also by noticing things which were mentioned long ago in scripture, for which there does not seem to have been any way for those in that time to have known. Further after years of reading, noticing a harmony, an agreement between things written over hundreds or thousands of years by various people. Unlike those living during Christ's first visit who believed by the miracles they saw, our faith, the faith of those of us living after Christ, who have committed to Christ, is not by sight as mentioned in 2 Cor. 5:7, Heb. 11:1 and Rom. 10:17. Should we then require the miraculous now as the Pharisees did, to believe that Christ is soon to return? Or are a series of unusual events prophesied long ago, which fit the prophesied descriptions, enough to believe?

Acts 2:16&20 may lead some people to believe that the blood moons seen in 69AD – 71AD are the ones fulfilling the prophecies, and not the sets in 2014 and 2015. I think we will find that this is correct in part, however not wholly accurate. The events around 70AD are more likely similar to a preview, than the main event itself. They were fulfilling in part but not in whole.

> October 18th 69AD there was a partial lunar eclipse.
> April 14th 70AD there was a penumbral lunar eclipse.
> September 9th 70AD there was a penumbral lunar eclipse.
> October 8th 70AD there was a penumbral lunar eclipse.
> October 8th 71AD there was a penumbral lunar eclipse.

The 70AD events did not occur during the time period mentioned in Daniel 12:4, the later Industrial Age and the Information Age. Israel was not born or reborn in one day in 70AD as it was in 1948, as per Jesus' prophesy. Jesus refers to the rapture in Matthew 24:28, 30-31. History has not mentioned a rapture in 70AD. Jesus mentioned God's wrath being poured out in Matthew 24:29&30 and Revelation 6:13-17. I am not aware that history has mentioned fire and brimstone falling in or about 70AD killing most or all people on earth. Nor was there seen in the aforementioned list of blood moons during or near 70AD, even one total lunar eclipse, as required by Revelation 6:12 "the whole moon became like blood" (NASB). There were similar events around 70AD; however, they did not completely fulfill the prophecies. Again 70AD seems to have been like a preview, a partial fulfilling. The 2014-2015 blood moons are almost certainly a precursor to the main event.

"…and there will be terrors and great signs from heaven." (Luke 21:11 NASB)

A Perspective of Matthew 24 to Revelation Chapters 1-8. The Context. "The Revelation of Jesus Christ, which God gave Him to show to His bond-servants, ...to His bond servant John." (NASB) Rev.1:1 "John to the seven Churches..." Rev. 1:4. (NASB) Then in Rev. 1:12 John says that he sees seven golden lampstands. In Rev. 1:20 Christ explains that these golden lampstands are the seven churches and then starts addressing the churches in Rev. chap. 2.

An offence – a sin committed, is mentioned "...you have left your first love." Rev. 2:4. (NASB) Apparently most of those of the church of Ephesus are not making Christ the focus of their lives. The consequence - "...**repent** and do the deeds you did at first; or else I am coming to you, and will **remove your lampstand** out of its place – unless your **repent**." Rev.2:5. (NASB) In Rev. 2:7 Christ mentions that the one who "overcomes" will be granted "the Paradise of God".

The church of Smyrna is being "**tested**" – tormented by "the devil". This church is told to "...**Be faithful until death, ...**" Rev.2:10 (NASB), to "**overcome**" the testing and remain faithful.

In Rev. 2:12-16 the church at Pergamum has evidently not denied Christ – "...you hold fast My name, ..."Rev. 2:13 (NASB), yet there are "...some who hold the teachings of Balaam,..." Rev. 2:14 and false teachings of "Balak" & "the Nicolaitans.". They are told to "**repent**".

Christ acknowledges the works of the church at Thyatira and their steadfast faith. However, they have "tolerated" – they have not opposed – acts of idolatry, apparently within their church. Followers of the idolatry of "Jezebel" are told to "**repent**", three times. The church at Thyatira is also told to "hold fast" and "overcome". Rev. 2:18-29

Rev. 3:1-6 is to the church at Sardis, who seem think they are Christians – "you are alive"; however, Christ says they are "dead" and mentions their actions. We can be known by our actions. Christ tells them "**repent**", "**wake up**", "...and I will not erase his name from the book of life, and I will confess his name before My Father..." Rev. 3:5. (NASB) Are these true Christians who are have now rejected Christianity? Unlikely; they probably had not understood a commitment to Christ. In Rev. 3:3 Christ says "I will come like a thief…" Rev. 3:3. (NASB) Being "dead" and being caught by a "thief" are normally not associated with committed Christians.

The church at Philadelphia seems to be fairly strong (Rev. 3:7-12). "…you have a little power, and have kept My word, and have not denied My name." Rev. 3:8 (NASB) "…you have kept the word of My perseverance…" Rev. 3:10 NASB). They are told to "hold fast" and overcome. The seventh church, the church at Laodicea, is told "…you are neither cold nor hot; …I will spit you out of My mouth." Rev. 3:15&16. (NASB) Christ says of them (or most) that they are "poor", "wretched" and naked. These types of comments are often used of those who have not committed to Christ. Then Christ says, "Behold, I stand at the door and knock; if anyone hears My voice and opens the door, I will come in to him, and dine with him, and he with Me." Rev. 3:20. (NASB) This is an invitation – to commit their lives to Christ – to become Christians. Is this a church in which many, or most of those of the congregation are actually not Christians?

Where are these people – churches? John is writing this on earth, after Christ's resurrection. In Rev. 4:2 John says he sees a door open in heaven and then is told "Come up here, …". Where was John until this time? Almost certainly on earth on the island of Patmos, until this point. In Rev. chapters 1-3 there is nothing to suggest the church is in heaven. If in heaven they would not be told to repent. There has been no mention of the rapture. In Rev. 2:14, 15, 20-22 idolatry with Balaam, Balak, the teachings of the Nicolaitans and Jezebel are mentioned. There will not be any false teaching in heaven. These teachings are being mentioned involving the church and therefore false teachings involving Christ. As previously mentioned, Christ may be including falsely teaching with false Christs the, white horse (Rev. 6:2 & Matt. 24:4-5). In Rev.2:16 the letter to the church in Pergamum Christ mentions "war" and "sword", which Christ also mentions as the red horse in Rev. 6:4 & Matt. 24:6. In Rev. 2:23 Christ mentions "pestilence", which He also mentions in Rev. 6:8, in describing the ashen horse. Martyrdom is mentioned in Rev. 2:10 Rev. 6:9-11 & Matt. 24:9. These churches in Rev. chapters 1-3 are almost certainly on earth before the Great Tribulation and are being warned to repent to avoid suffering from the seals to be opened.

To whom is Revelation chapters 1-3 speaking? It seems that it is addressed to everyone from the time John wrote the book of Revelation and forward. However, Rev. 2:22 states "Behold, I will cast her upon a bed of *sickness*, and those who commit adultery with her into **great tribulation**, unless they repent of her deeds." (NASB, EM) There is only one Great Tribulation. Specifically, Christ is most likely primarily speaking to those who are alive soon before the Great Tribulation. Specifically, in Rev. 2:22, the "great tribulation" Christ is speaking of is almost certainly the last portion of the Great Tribulation as it is His wrath, which He has mentioned (Rev. 2:5, 16, 22, 23; 3:16). When Christ mentions "the hour of testing" in Rev. 3:10, it is almost certainly the last portion of the Great Tribulation He is speaking of. In these passages we have seen idolatry – likely as false Christs, War the red horse, pestilence from the ashen horse and in Rev. 2:22 the "great tribulation". This sounds like some of the five seals of Rev. 6 and then the Great Tribulation, as laid out earlier. Those who have not accepted Christ and those who thought they were Christians but are not true Christians will experience all of the plagues of the book of Revelation.

Following Rev. 1-3 John says "After these things..." Rev. 4:1 (NASB); therefore events are most likely in chronological order. John then mentions being called to heaven, being told ..."Come up here, ..." Rev. 4:1 (NASB). Rev. 4:2 "Immediately I was in the Spirit; and behold, a throne was standing in heaven, and One sitting on the throne." (NASB) John is now in heaven, either in body or in spirit and prior to chapter 4 on earth. In Rev. chapters 4 & 5, which take place in heaven, there does not seem to be any mention of the golden lampstands, which represent the churches. Rev. 4:4, 10 & 5:8, occur in heaven, where John sees twenty-four elders sitting on twenty-four thrones. The text does not tell who they are. There is no mention that they were raptured. Who these Christian elders are would only be a guess. There is no evidence from Revelation chapters 1 through 5 that the rapture has occurred or that all Christians of that time are in heaven. The context seems to suggest that the church has been warned (Rev. chap. 1-3), all people have been given notice to "repent", to "hold fast" to Christ and to "overcome" sin. Then ("After these things…") Revelation chapters 4 & 5 give a glorious mention at God's throne, heaven, praise to God and the mention of seals to be opened. Seals which when opened tell us what those on earth are about to experience. Rev. 5:9 …"Worthy art Thou to take the book, and break its seals; …" (NASB) Rev. 5:11 "Then…

In Rev. 6 we are told of false Christs, war, and famine. Suffering increases, and there are pestilence, wild beasts, earthquakes and martyrdom. The Blood Moons then occur "after" the suffering and martyrdom "of those days". After which many fall away, there is lawlessness and the Gospel is preached to all nations. Then the end – the Great Tribulation – will come. The anti-Christ – the Abomination of Desolation – enters the temple, triggering the Great Tribulation (Matt. 24:21). Christians are now persecuted for 1,335 days (?), the first portion of the Great Tribulation. (The rapture occurs between the moon turning to blood in Rev. 6:12 and the stars falling from the sky in Rev. 6:13.) The rapture is indicated by Christ being seen in the clouds and angels finding Christians in Matt. 24:27&28.

After Rev. 6 it is almost certain that we see a jump into heaven in Rev. chapters 7&8, describing what is occurring there. "After this I saw four angels standing at the four corners of the earth, holding back the four winds of the earth, so that no wind should blow on the earth or on the sea or on any tree" Rev. 7:1. (NASB) It is highly probable that Rev. 8:1 is occurring at the same time. "And when He broke the seventh seal, there was silence in heaven for about half an hour." Rev. 8:1. (NASB) Rev. 8:2-4 continues speaking of seven angels, prayers of saints and incense. Almost certainly at the same time in Revelation 7:3-8, 144,000 Jews are being sealed for protection as they will be preaching during the last portion of the Great Tribulation. At the same time in Rev. 7:9-17 we are told of a "great multitude praising God in heaven. We are told in Rev. 7:14 "… These are the ones who come out of the great tribulation, and they have washed their robes and made them white in the blood of the Lamb." (NASB, EM)

The rapture has just occurred. Then it appears that a time of a half hour occurs, during which wind on the earth stops blowing, the 144,000 are sealed, those raptured are found in heaven and prayers, incense and angels are mentioned. The jump back and forth form Revelation chapter 7 and Revelation 8 may have seemed odd. Yet notice something in common between Matthew 24, Revelation 6 and Revelation 8, which occurs next in order.

Matthew 24:29 "...**AND THE STARS WILL FALL from the sky** ..." (NASB, EM)

Revelation 6:12&13 "… and there was a great earthquake; … 13 and the **stars of the sky fell** to the earth, as a fig tree casts its unripe figs when shaken by a great wind." (NASB, EM)

Revelation 8:5, 7, 8, 10, 11. 5 "And the angel took the censer; and filled it with the **fire** of the altar **and threw it to the earth**; and there followed peals of thunder and sounds and flashes of lightning and an earthquake. 8:7 "… and there came hail and **fire,** …" 8:8 "… and *something* like a great **mountain burning** with **fire… thrown to the earth…** 10 …and a great **star fell from heaven, burning like a torch** … 11 and the name of the **star is called Wormwood;**…"(NASB, EM)

All three passages, Matt. 24:29, Rev. 6:13 and Rev. 8:5,7,8,10,&11 are all talking about luminous objects – shooting stars - fire and brimstone – meteorites – meteors and one or more asteroids – a great Mountain, all which can describe the stars falling. Revelation 8:5, 7, 8, 10 & 11 most likely take off with the same event mentioned in Matt. 24:29 and Rev. 6:13, stars falling from the sky. The rapture occurs, about thirty minutes seem to pass during which Christians are received into heaven, taken "out of" the Great Tribulation, the 144,000 are sealed and the prayers, incense and angels are mentioned. Then the stars mentioned in Matthew 24:29, Revelation 6:13 and Revelation 8:5, 7, 8, 10 & 11 start falling from the sky. After which other types of wrath come upon the earth, from Revelation chapter 8 and on.

Next - The Third Parallel View compares Matthew 24 with Revelation chapters 1 through 8 in brief. To understand, read the first few verses in the left column on the first page. Then a few verses in the right-hand column of the first page. Then move to the second page, the left-hand column and then a few verses from the right-hand column on the second page, the right-hand page, always looking for the same topics. Then of course go back to the left page to the next few passages, and repeat. As you read down the two pages together, events proceed in time from top to bottom. If you are reading by E-book you may need to jump back and forth between the two pages.

The Third Parallel View

Matt. 24:3 "… Tell us, <u>when</u> will these <u>things</u> be, and <u>what</u> will be the <u>sign</u> of <u>Your coming</u>, and the <u>end of the age</u>?" (NASB, EM)

The Seals Opened Now Occur

1914-2030? Matt. 24:4-9 **False Christs, Wars, Famines, Earthquakes, Suffering Increases** and **Martyrdom.** 2014-2015 Four Blood Moons. Matt. 24:29 "… **THE SUN WILL BE DARKENDED, AND THE MOON WILL NOT GIVE ITS LIGHT,..** (NASB,EM) Now THE Temple is rebuilt. Israel signs a 7 yr. treaty. Matt. 24:15 The gospel is taught throughout the world. Then – "the end" –the Great Tribulation soon starts.

The sacrifices have now been carried out for 3 ½ years.

2025? **The Great Tribulation starts** as The Abomination of Desolation enters THE Temple. Matt. 24:15-21 2025-2028? Christians & Jews are persecuted, hunted and killed for Approx. 3 ½ years. Matt. 24:16-26 Matt. 24:27-28

2028-2030? **The Rapture** occurs approx. 7 years after the sacrifices were restarted. Christ is seen in the sky- Matt. 24:27&30. Angels participate in the rapture – Matt. 24:28&31 *Approximately one half hour passes between the Rapture and Wrath?* Rev. 8:1

****

"**AND THE STARS WILL FALL FROM THE SKY,** … Matt. 24:29 (NASB,EM) "…<u>then all the tribes of the earth will mourn</u>,… Matt. 24:30 (NASB,EM)

Revelation 6

The Seals Opened Now Occur

1914-2030? The **White Horse, Red Horse, Black Horse, Ashen Horse, pestilence** and **Martyrdom.** Revelation 6:1-11

2014-2015 Rev. 6:12 "…**the sun became black as sackcloth made of hair, and the whole moon became like** blood;…" (NASB,EM)

Revelation 6 is now silent No mention of the first portion Of the Great Tribulation

and the stars of the sky fell to the earth,… Rev. 6:13 (NASB,EM) <u>Kings, great men, commanders, the rich, the strong, slaves and free now hide in caves and among rocks and call out due to wrath.</u> Rev. 6:15-17

The Third Parallel View

*Warnings & encouragement **before the seals are opened*** Revelation 1-5 & 7 To the Church 70 A.D. & on. Primarily 1914 – 2028? In Rev. 1, John is on the island of Patmos. The 7 churches are represented by 7 golden lampstands. In Rev. 2-3, Christ speaks of **Idols – false teaching, war, pestilence &** suffering **great tribulation** therefore - "**repent**", to "overcome" sin and "**hold fast**". Rev. 4-5 John sees a door open in heaven and is told to come up. God is being given praise and Christ – the Lamb will open the seals found starting in Rev. 6:1, they are opened.

*Revelation 7 is now silent
No mention of the first portion
Of the Great Tribulation*

One half hour of events occurring after the rapture and before God's wrath?
****

2028-2030? The rapture has just occurred.
Rev. 7:1 **All wind on earth has stopped.**
Rev. 7:2-8 144,000 Jews who will preach during the 2nd portion of the Great Trib. are being sealed. Rev. 7:9-17 there is a great multitude "…who come out of the great tribulation…" Rev. 7:14 (NASB)

Revelation 8

*Revelation 8 is now silent.
No mention of the first portion
Of the Great Tribulation*

Thirty minutes of time between the rapture and wrath –the stars falling from the sky?
****

2028-2030? The rapture has just occurred.
Rev. 8:1 **…,there was silence in heaven for about half an hour.**" (NASB,EM) The prayers of saints are given to God. Prayer and Praise.

2028 – 2030?
Rev. 8:5-11 In vs. **fire is thrown to earth** (fire and brimstone?) Vs. 7 more **fire** & hail. Vs.8 a **mountain** (an asteroid?) **burning thrown to earth**. Vs. 10 a **star** (an asteroid?) **falls to earth**. Vs. 11 the stars name is "**Wormwood**". This sounds just like Mat. 24:29 and Rev. 6:13. Rev. 8:5-11 seems to pick up with the same topic of stars falling from the sky in Matt. 24:29 & Rev. 6:13.

18 Not Destined for Wrath: It Is Not a Post-Tribulation Rapture

I can hear some of you saying, "But God has not destined us for wrath, so there can't be a mid–tribulation rapture." You are correct that we are not appointed to wrath, and the answer may not have been clear earlier. "For God has not destined us for wrath, but for obtaining salvation through our Lord Jesus Christ, …" (1 Thess. 5:9, NASB). However, some things might need to be clarified in order for us to understand.

"…with regard to the coming of our Lord Jesus Christ and our gathering together to Him, 2 … the day of the Lord … 3 … will not come unless … the man of lawlessness is revealed, the son of destruction, 4 who opposes and exalts himself … … he takes his seat in the temple of God, displaying himself as being God." (2 Thess. 2:1–4, NASB). This man of lawlessness is the abomination of desolation, and the passage says he will be revealed, seen. Further, he "displays himself," makes himself known. To whom? The epistle of 2 Thessalonians was written to Christians; therefore he is made known to those of us who have made Christ Lord and Savior, and possibly to all people.

This has been stated in other words, as Jesus speaks to those who follow Him: " …when you see the ABOMINATION OF DESOLATION …" (Matt. 24:15, NASB, EM) and "… they will set up the abomination of desolation." (Dan. 11:31, NASB). The first part of the Great Tribulation is Satan, roaring like a lion, pouring out his wrath. Then immediately after Christ returns for the rapture, God's wrath is poured out. Christians miss God's wrath, which is the last part of the Great Tribulation.

It is true that we are not appointed to wrath, and this has been an issue of confusion. Jesus and Daniel specify "when you see the abomination of desolation." Daniel and Jesus were talking to followers of God, followers of Christ, us. The abomination of desolation will most likely be seen on TV by most of us.

Most people seem to think that when the abomination of desolation, also referred to as the Antichrist, comes on the scene, God pours out wrath. Not true; that happens in the last portion. In this way, Christians do go through the first half of the Great Tribulation but do not experience God's wrath which is poured in the second portion, on those who rejected Him. Hopefully this is clear.

It Is Not a Post–Great Tribulation Rapture

We can have confidence that it is not a post–Great Tribulation rapture. The rapture will not come at the end of the Great Tribulation. In 1 Thessalonians 5:9 we are told Christians will not experience God's wrath, and the last half or portion of the Great Tribulation is God's wrath. Therefore, the rapture has already occurred before God's wrath is poured out.

Rev. 6:1-12 and Matt.24:4-14 describe what is happening in the last days leading up to the beginning of the Great Tribulation. Matt. 24:15-26 describes some of the suffering of Christians in the first portion of the Great Tribulation. Matt. 24:27-31 and Rev.7:9-14 mention the rapture. Rev. 6:13-17 and Matt. 24:29&30 mention the beginning of God's wrath. Then Rev. chapters 8-17&18 describe the suffering during the last portion of the Great Tribulation, of those who did not accept Christ.

Reading from Revelation 8 through chapter 18, it is hard to believe that anyone could live through God's wrath. Jesus said it will be just as it was in the days of Noah and Lot, in which no one but God's elect were saved. In addition Jesus speaks of God's elect in Matthew 24:22, telling us that unless God shortened Christians' time on earth, no Christian life would be saved. However, due to God's grace, some people who reject having the mark of the beast placed on their hand or forehead may be saved if they accept Christ. The number saved would seem to be few. It is almost certainly not a post-Great Tribulation rapture.

19   He Who Restrains

Since it may not have been clear from the previous passages, the teaching that the Holy Spirit is restraining the anti-Christ until Christians are raptured will now be addressed. What about he who now restrains? Isn't it the Holy Spirit? "And you know what <u>restrains him now</u>, so that *in his time he may be* **revealed.** 7 For *the mystery of lawlessness is already at work*; only **he** <u>who now restrains will do so until</u> **he** *is taken out of the way.* 8 And **then** *that lawless one will be revealed* <u>whom the Lord will slay</u> with the breath of His mouth and bring an end by the appearance of His coming;" (2 Thess. 2:6–8, NASB, EM). Please notice that neither "he" is capitalized in 2 Thess. 2:7, through perhaps one should be.

This is a bit difficult, as many, many of us have been told the "restrainer" is the Holy Spirit within us. We have been told when "**he** is taken out of the way," that is when the rapture occurs. The Holy Spirit within us will no longer be on earth, restraining the Antichrist.

Let me offer a different view. Consider "…when you **see** the abomination of desolation …" (Matt. 24:15, NASB). [Jesus, speaking to his disciples, including us, says we will see the abomination of desolation.] "…and the man of lawlessness is revealed … 4 … **he** takes his seat in the temple of God …" (2 Thess. 2:3, 4, NASB, EM). [Who takes a seat in the temple? The abomination of desolation does, who is the man of lawlessness.]

So again, we Christians are alive when the abomination of desolation appears, approximately three and a half years after the sacrifices are started. We see the Antichrist, the abomination of desolation, desecrate the temple while the Holy Spirit resides in us; the Holy Spirit has not left the earth.

Abraham believed God and God said that Abraham was given righteousness due to his belief (James 2:23). King David prayed that the Holy Spirit not be taken away from him in Psalm 51:11. Job must also have believed God, as Abraham and King David did, otherwise why would Job have remained faithful to God under such torment. Job was likely being tormented by

Satan while the Holy Spirit lived within him. Why should it then be necessary that the Holy Spirit to be taken out of the earth for Satan or the man of lawlessness to be revealed as something similar has already occurred with Job on earth?

Job 1 and 2 speak of God limiting what the lawless one—Satan—can do. In 2 Thessalonians 2:6, we are told, "And you know what restrains him now, so that in his time he may be revealed" (NASB). Job seems to be speaking of God—God the Father—restraining and here in 2 Thess. God is also restraining.

In the same epistle, 2 Thessalonians 3:3: "But the **Lord** is faithful, and **He** will strengthen and **protect you from the evil one.**" (NASB, EM). Again, this sounds like God the Father. That God will protect Christians during the first half of the Great Tribulation. However, this does not mean Christians will not suffer or be martyred.

In 2 Thessalonians 3:3 and Job 1 and 2, God, apparently God the Father, is the one restraining. Why then does it say in 2 Thessalonians 2:7 that "…**he** who now restrains will do so until **he** is taken out of the way." (NASB, EM).

Please consider the possibility that the second "he" in 2 Thess. 2:7 speaks of Satan. Therefore **He**—God—will restrain (limit), until **he**—Satan—is taken out of the way, sent to fiery hell.

In the next verse it says, "And then that **lawless one** will **be revealed** _whom the lord will slay_ … _by the appearance of His coming;_" (2 Thess. 2:8, NASB, EM). [Viewed this way, God the Father has always been restraining.] "And you know what **restrains him now, …**" (2 Thess. 2:6, NASB, EM). God the Father has been restraining him—Satan and God will continue to restrain.

"…bring to an end by the appearance of His coming;" (2 Thess. 2:8, NASB). When Christ returns at the very end of the Great Tribulation, Christ will slay Satan—the abomination of desolation—at Christ's appearance. Christ will put an end to Satan when Christ returns at the very end. In the meantime God the Father continues to restrain the abomination of desolation.

The abomination of desolation, the man of lawlessness, the son of destruction, a despicable person, all the same individual, all seem to be empowered by Satan. The only twist might be if Revelation 13:12–14 is stating this man of sin, the abomination of desolation, is killed and his body is then possessed by Satan.

"And I saw heaven opened; and behold, a white horse, and He who sat upon it is called Faithful and True; and in righteousness He judges and wages war. ... 13 And He is clothed with a robe dipped in blood; and His name is called The Word of God ... 20 And the beast was seized, and with him the false prophet who performed the signs in his presence, by which he deceived those who had received the mark of the beast and those who worshiped his image; these two were thrown alive into the lake of fire which burns with brimstone." (Rev. 19:11,13,20, NASB).

How can that be? In 2 Thessalonians 2:8, "slay" and "bring to an end" are mentioned, yet here it says they are thrown into a lake of fire? "And death and Hades were thrown into the lake of fire. "... This is **the second death**, the lake of fire." (Rev. 20:14, NASB, EM). So the abomination of desolation, who seems to be spoken of in Revelation 6:8 as " ...Death; and Hades was following with him ..." (NASB), was thrown into the lake of fire, the second death. In 2 Thessalonians 2:7, "... he is taken out of the way." (NASB, EM) does not seem to be the Holy Spirit, but Satan as mentioned in Revelation 20:14.

"...with regard to the coming of our Lord Jesus Christ, and our gathering together to Him, ...3 it will not come unless ... the man of lawlessness is revealed ... 8 And when that lawless one will be revealed whom the Lord will slay with the breath of His mouth and bring to an end by the appearance of His coming;" (2 Thess. 2:1, 3, 8, NASB). This slaying of Satan occurs upon Christ's return at the very end of the Great Tribulation. Satan is the one taken out of the way, and God is protecting Christians until he is.

Phrases from Revelation give us context.

1:1: "The Revelation of Jesus Christ, …"

1:5: "…and from Jesus Christ, …"

1:6 "and He has made us to be a kingdom, priests to His God and Father; …"

1:8: 'I am the Alpha and the Omega", says the Lord God, ..."

1:17: '…Do not be afraid; I am the first and the last,"

2:18: '…The Son of God, who has eyes like a flame of fire …"

2:10: 'Do not fear what you are about to suffer. Behold, the devil is about to cast some of you into prison, that you may be tested, …"

3:10: "Because you have kept the word of My perseverance, **I also will keep you from the hour of testing**, that hour which is about to come upon the whole world, to test those who dwell upon earth."(NASB, EM).

Here Christ states He "will keep you from the hour of testing" (NASB) which almost certainly is the last half of the Great Tribulation, which is God's wrath. No mention is made here that the Holy Spirit is then restraining.

If Christians who have been convinced that it will be a pre-tribulation rapture see the abomination of desolation, some may think they have missed the rapture. This could unfortunately lead to crippling depression, at one of the worst times possible for that to happen. Even if some do not agree now, it might be best for them to at least understand the mid-tribulation view so that they may remain composed if things don't go as they expect.

20 Complementary Passages: Thinking about the Probability

"And as He was sitting on the Mount of Olives, the disciples came to Him privately, saying, "Tell us, **when** will **these things be**, and **what** will be the **sign** of **Your coming**, and of the **end of the age?**"(Matt. 24:3, NASB, EM).

1914—World War I begins.

"But as for you, Daniel, conceal these words and seal up the book until the end of time; <u>many will back and forth, ...</u>" (Dan. 12:4, NASB, EM).

Transportation makes advances and people from many nations, rush into Europe and other parts of the world during World War I – 1914 and the end times begin.

"And Jesus answered and said to them, "See to it that **no one misleads you.** 5 "For **many will come in My name**, saying, '**I am the Christ, 'and will mislead many.**" (Matt. 24:4–5, NASB, EM).

"And I saw when the Lamb broke one of the seven seals, and I heard one of the four living creatures saying as with a voice of thunder, "Come." 2 And I looked, and behold, a **white horse**, and he who sat on it **had a bow**; and a **crown was given** to him; and he went out **conquering, and to conquer.**" (Rev. 6:1–2, NASB, EM).

Matthew 24:4-5 and Revelation 6:2 both speak of false Christs.

"And just as it happened in the days of Noah, so it shall be also in the days of the Son of Man: 27 they were eating, they were drinking, they were marrying, they were being given in marriage, until the day that Noah entered the ark, and the flood came and destroyed them all." (Luke 17:26–27, NASB).

Life for many people goes on as normal it seems, including war.

1930's—This date is only being mentioned to give the concept of the passage of time. The events of this section also likely started in 1914.

"And you will be hearing of **wars** and rumors of **wars**; see that you are not frightened, for *those things* must take place, but that is not yet the end." (Matt. 24:6, NASB, EM).

"And another, a **red** horse, went out; and to him who sat on it, <u>it was granted</u> to **take peace from the earth**, and that **men should slay one another**; and a **great sword** was <u>given</u> to him." (Rev. 6:4, NASB, EM).

Matthew 24:6 and Revelation 6:4 both speak of war.

1939—World War II begins.

1940s—This is still the time period mentioned in Daniel 12:4 of people rushing. The latter part of the Industrial Age is still ongoing.

"For nation will rise against nation, and kingdom against kingdom and in various places there will be **famines** and earthquakes." (Matt. 24:7, NASB, EM).

"And when He broke the third seal, I heard the third living creature saying, "Come." And I looked, and behold, a **black** horse; and he who sat on it had a **pair of scales** in his hand. 6 And I heard as it were a voice in the center of the four living creatures saying, "**A quart of wheat for a denarius**, and **three quarts of barley for a denarius**; and <u>do not harm the oil and the wine.</u>" (Rev. 6:5-6, NASB, EM)<u>.</u>

The scales weigh the grain paid for a day's wage; this is famine. Both Matthew 24:7 and Revelation 6:5 speak of famine.

"And when He broke the fourth seal, I heard the voice of the fourth living creature saying "Come." 8 And I looked, and behold, an **ashen** horse; and he who sat on it had the name **Death**; and **Hades** was **following** with him. And **authority was given to them** over a **fourth** of the **earth**, to **kill** with **sword** and with **famine** and with **pestilence** and by the **wild beasts** of the earth." (Rev. 6:7-8, NASB, EM).

"But all these **things** are *merely* the **beginning** of **birth pangs**." (Matt. 24:8, NASB, EM).

Like the pain of physical childbirth, these pangs increase in intensity. War, famine, pestilence, earthquakes, and wild beasts increase suffering and death. The ability of weapons of war to kill during World War I was greatly increased over previous wars. This seems to indicate that the ashen horse – birth pang likely started about 1914.

"Now learn the parable from **the fig tree: when** its branch has already become tender, **and puts forth its leaves**, you **know** that summer is near; 33 even so you too, **when** you **see all these things, recognize** that **HE** is near, right at the door." (Matt. 24:32–33, NASB, EM).

1948—Israel is reborn in May. "Near" is relative term in time for a prophecy made nearly two thousand years prior to 1948. In context, seventy or eighty years (the span of a generation, per Psalm 90:10) is near.

1950 (approximately)–2015, and continuing until the first half of the Great Tribulation is over.

"And when He broke the fifth seal, I saw underneath the altar the **souls** of those who had been **slain because of the word of God**, and because of the **testimony which they had maintained**; 10 and **they** cried out with a loud voice, saying, "How' long, O Lord, holy and true, wilt Thou refrain from judging and avenging **our blood** on those who dwell on the earth?" 11 And there was given to each of them a **white robe**; and they were told that **they** should rest for a little while longer, **until** the **number** of **their fellow servants** and **their brethren who were to be killed even as they had been** should be **completed** also." (Rev.6:9-11, NASB, EM).

"**Then** they will **deliver you to tribulation,** and will **kill you,** and you will be **hated** by all nations on **account of My name.**" (Matt. 24:9, NASB, EM).

There have been more Christians killed martyred since about 1950 than in all prior history. In fact, those who have seen nothing else have likely seen video of Christians in orange jumpsuits, killed by ISIS.

1990 (approximately) the Information Age begins.

2001 the 9/11 terrorist attacks occur. This is almost certainly a harbinger, a warning, as Rabbi Jonathan Chan explains on his DVD *Isaiah 9:10.* Producer – Joseph Farah, Production Company –WND Films, 12/3/2012.

April 15, 2014–September 28, 2015—the set of four blood moons.

"… and there will be terrors and great signs from heaven." (Luke 21:11, NASB)

"And there will be signs in sun and moon and stars, and upon the earth dismay among nations, in perplexity at the roaring of the sea and the waves," (Luke 21:25, NASB)

Matt. 24:29, a split verse, follows Matt. 24:9. This first half of Matt. 24:29 is split from the second half by approximately seven to fourteen years.

"But immediately **after** the **tribulation** of **those days THE SUN WILL BE DARKENED, AND THE MOON WILL NOT GIVE ITS LIGHT**, …"(Matt. 24:29, NASB, EM).

Next Revelation 6:12–13 are split primarily by "and" and also by a semicolon. The first portion of Rev. 6:12 occurs (then a split) then approximately seven to eleven years go by and then Rev. 6:13 will occur.

"And I looked when He broke the sixth seal, and there was a great earthquake; and the **sun became black as sackcloth made of hair, and the <u>whole</u> moon became like blood.**" (Rev.6:12, NASB, EM).

This is the only set of four blood moons in this century or last in which all the blood moons are *total* lunar eclipses and occur during the time mentioned by Daniel and Jesus. Also, these blood moons all occurred during Jewish High Holy Days.

"But in **those days, after <u>that</u> tribulation, THE SUN WILL BE DARKENED, AND THE MOON WILL NOT GIVE ITS LIGHT,**" (Mark 13:24, NASB, EM).

"The sun will be turned into darkness, and the moon into blood, <u>before</u> the great and awesome day of the Lord comes." (Joel 2:31, NASB, EM).

The awesome day of the Lord is His wrath in the last part of the Great Tribulation.

Matthew 24:9 addresses tribulation and martyrdom, and Matthew 24:29, a split verse, follows, which talks about the moon turning to blood. These are almost certainly the blood moons seen in 2014–2015. "And **<u>at that</u> <u>time</u> many will fall away** and will **deliver up one another** and hate one another." (Matt.24:10, NASB, EM).

These might actually be Christians; however, they may be those spoken of in Jude 4: "For certain persons have crept in unnoticed, … who turn the grace of our God into licentiousness and deny our only Master and Lord, Jesus Christ." (NASB).

"…with regard to the coming of our Lord Jesus Christ, and our gathering together to Him, … 3 Let no one in any way deceive you, for it will not come unless the apostasy comes first, …" (2 Thess. 2:1, 3, NASB). The word *apostasy* refers to those who give up the Christian faith or who appeared to be Christians but stopped going to Church. Note the falling away comes before Christ's return for the Church.

"**<u>And</u>** many false prophets will arise, and will mislead many. 12 "**<u>And</u> because lawlessness is increased, most people's love will grow cold.**" (Matt. 24:11–12, NASB, EM).

Matthew 24:10 said "**at that time**," which is likely about the time of the 2014-2015 blood moons. The mention of "and" in Matthew 24:11–12 likely indicates that the false prophets and the love of most growing cold, starts increasing at the same time period as the blood moons.

Revelation 6 has been covering the same topics in the same order but now stops at a split verse, skipping approximately seven to eleven years. Revelation 6 picks up again with the last half of Matthew 24:29, a split verse.

This time period of seven to fourteen years is estimated. The three and a half years of sacrifices must be an almost exact three and a half years.

2015–2023 (estimated)

"But the one who endures to the end, he shall be saved. 14 "And **this gospel of the kingdom** shall be **preached in the whole world** for a witness to all the nations, and **then the end shall come**. 15 "Therefore when you see the ABOMINATION OF DESOLATION which was spoken of through Daniel the prophet, standing in **the holy place** …" (Matt. 24:13-15, NASB, EM).

"The end" is almost definitely the Great Tribulation. Most of the world has heard the gospel through missionaries, the Bible translated into their language, TV, or radio. The preaching of the gospel might be accelerated by technology. A computer program that uses the spoken language of a culture to translate the Bible could be downloaded into cost-effective cell phones. The preaching of the gospel must be nearing completion. We can have confidence that the phrase "endures to the end" does not mean lives to the end, but maintains their faith in Christ until the rapture.

In Matthew 24:15, there is mention of the Holy place, which is the Temple in Jerusalem. It was destroyed approximately two thousand years ago. During our time, 1916–2027 approximately, the temple must be rebuilt. If not, the abomination of desolation cannot be standing in the holy place, being set up.

2017–2023 - the treaty will likely occur within this time period.

"And he will make a firm covenant with the many for one week, but in the middle of the week he will put a stop to sacrifice and grain offering; and on the wing of abominations *will come* one who makes desolate, even until a complete destruction, one that is decreed, is poured out on the one who makes desolate." (Dan. 9:27, NASB).

The covenant—peace treaty—is made. The sacrifices are started and run for three and a half years. The abomination of desolation then stops the sacrifices and desecrates the temple. The first half or portion of the Great Tribulation starts. The one who makes desolate is almost certainly the abomination of desolation, the Antichrist. God/Christ is the one who will pour out wrath, or destruction on the abomination of desolation, beginning at the end of the Great Tribulation.

In Daniel 9:27 a covenant or (seven year) treaty is signed. Israel must either enter into a treaty in hopes of avoiding annihilation, or must engage in war to defend its existence and then sign a treaty. This could occur as soon as 2017 or closer to 2023.

The text states that this treaty lasts for one week. It is highly unlikely that this would be a literal seven-day week. Greater minds have concluded that this is a seven-year period. The treaty is broken by the abomination of desolation and stops the Jewish sacrifices in the Temple. See Alpha News Daily, www.theprophecies.com/Warning%2014%20Coming%20 Peace%20Plan.html; 3/28/2016 Chuck Missler: Koinonia House site, "Are We Living In The Last Days," www.areweilivinginthelastdays.com/article/ gogmagog/gogmagog.htm; Mark Blitz, www.wnd.com/2015/09/is-7-year-biblical-tribulation-about-to-start/). 3/28/2016

2022–2027 (approximately)—the Great Tribulation starts. If someone holds the position that the sacrifices are put to a stop by a peace treaty in the middle of the Great Tribulation, it presents a problem. In Matthew 24, Jesus explains the events in order, the only exception being the four blood moons in 24:29, which comes after 24:9, which is then in chronological order. Matthew 24:15 mentions the abomination of desolation going into the temple. Very soon after, Christ states in Matthew 24:21 that at that time, "then," the Great Tribulation will start.

The order of events in Matthew is as follows: There is a seven-year peace treaty, which is broken by the abomination of desolation in the middle of the treaty. The abomination of desolation is seen in the temple. The Great Tribulation starts and every one then suffers through the first part of the Great Tribulation. Then the rapture occurs, then comes the punishment of all who have not accepted Christ, launching the last half of the Great Tribulation, as stated in the last half of Matthew 24:29.

For Daniel 9:27 to agree with Matthew 24, it appears the treaty would have to be signed and the sacrifices made for three and a half years. Then the abomination of desolation would enter the temple in the middle of the treaty and put a stop to the sacrifices, which would be the beginning of the Great Tribulation. Others may hold the view that the Great Tribulation starts at the signing of the treaty. In Matthew 24, although not stated, Jesus seems to clearly indicate that the Great Tribulation starts in the middle of this treaty, not when the treaty is signed. Daniel 9:27 mentions that it is the middle of the week when the sacrifices are stopped. Daniel also mentions the wing of abominations. This sounds like the abomination of desolation standing in the holy place and putting an end to the sacrifices in the middle of the treaty. This in turn implies a start to the Great Tribulation in the middle of the treaty.

If the Great Tribulation starts in the middle of the treaty, how long is the second portion of the Great Tribulation? It would seem I should know, but not so, unfortunately. This does not mean the Great Tribulation does not start in the middle of the treaty. It simply means that the time the second portion lasts seems a bit elusive. The only people it will really be important to are those who do not accept Christ. The longer these poor souls are in the Great Tribulation, the more time they have to accept Christ, and the longer they delay judgment. However, it will be an extremely small amount of time in comparison to eternity and very few people if any are likely to except Christ during the last half.

"But when you see the ABOMINATION OF DESOLATION standing where it should not be (let the reader understand), then let those who are in Judea flee to the mountains. ... 19 "For those day will be a time of tribulation such as has not occurred since the beginning of the creation which God created, until now, and never shall." (Mark 13:14, 19, NASB). This is very similar to Matthew 24:15-21, except the abomination is described as "it."

"Come, my people, enter into your rooms, and close your doors behind you; hide for a little while, until indignation runs its course." (Isa. 26:20, NASB).

"Many will be **purged**, **purified** and **refined**; but the wicked will act wickedly, ..." (Dan. 12:10, NASB, EM).

Isaiah 26:20 and Daniel 12:10, sound like the same time period in Daniel 11:31-35: "And forces from him will arise, desecrate the sanctuary fortress, and do away with the regular sacrifice. And they will set up the abomination of desolation. 32 "And by smooth words he will turn to godlessness those who act wickedly toward the covenant, but the people who know their God will display strength and take action. 33 "And those who have insight among the people will give understanding to the many; yet they will fall by sword and by flame, by captivity and by plunder, for many days. 34 "Now when they fall they will be granted a little help, and many will join with them in hypocrisy. 35 "And **some** of those **who have insight** will fall, in order to **refine**, **purge** and make them **pure**, until **the end time**; because it is still to come at the appointed time."(NASB, EM). The "end time" stated here is almost certainly the last portion of the Great Tribulation, God's wrath.

As previously mentioned, Daniel 11:31–35 sounds very much like Matthew 24:15-16, 21–26:

"Therefore **when you see the ABOMINATION OF DESOLATION** which was spoken of through Daniel the prophet, **standing in the holy place** (let the reader understand), 16 **then** let those who are in Judea flee to the mountains; ... 21 for **then** there will be a **great tribulation**, such as has not occurred since the beginning of the world until now, nor ever shall. 22 "And unless those days had been cut short, no life would have been saved; but for the sake of the elect those days shall be cut short. 23 "**Then** if anyone says to you, 'Behold, here is the Christ,' or 'There He is,' do not believe him. 24 "For false Christs and false prophets will arise and will show great signs and wonders, so as to mislead, if possible, even the elect. 25 "Behold, I have told you in advance. 26 "If therefore they say to you, 'Behold, He is in the wilderness,' do not go forth, or, 'Behold, He is in the inner rooms,' do not believe them." (Matt. 24:15, 16, 21–26, NASB, EM).

Daniel 12:10 is most likely referring to the same events as Daniel 11:31–35, which begins with the abomination of desolation being set up and then talks about Christians in the first half of the Great Tribulation. Likewise, so does Matthew 24:15–26. This implies that Daniel 12:10 is referring to the same Christians found in Matthew 24:15–26.

"Many will be **purged**, **purified** and **refined**; but the wicked will act wickedly, and none of the wicked will understand, but **those who have insight will understand**. 11 "And from the time that the regular sacrifice is abolished, and the abomination of desolation is set up, *there will* be 1,290 days. 12 "How blessed is he who keeps waiting and attains to the 1,335 days!" (Dan. 12:10–12, NASB, EM).

If I have understood this correctly, the 1,290 days are the days of sacrifices, carried out until they are stopped by the abomination of desolation when he is set up in the Temple. Then the 1,335 days in Daniel 12:11 must refer to the time Christians will endure during the first half of the Great Tribulation, following the abomination of desolation being set up.

Daniel 12:12 talks of people who are blessed if they make it to the 1,335 days without denying Christ. The wicked, those who cling to being wicked, will not be blessed. Therefore, those who are blessed must be Christians who have made it to the end of the first half of the Great Tribulation without denying Christ, who are about to be raptured.

Yes, a question remains. "… **from the time** that the <u>regular sacrifice is abolished</u>, **and** the <u>abomination of desolation is set up</u>, *there will* be

1,290 days." (Dan.12:11, NASB, EM). This could be understood to mean that the regular sacrifice is abolished, and then, 1,290 days later, the abomination of desolation is set up. This does not seem to be the case. It seems to mean that from the time the sacrifices are started, until the time the sacrifices are stopped and the abomination of desolation is set up will be 1,290 days, in the middle of the treaty in Daniel 9:27. Stated another way, the passage seems to mean that both events, the sacrifices being carried out for 1,290 days at which time they are stopped **and** including the abomination of desolation is set up, is 1,290 days.

The end of the sacrifices and the abomination of desolation being where he should not be, are signals of the start of the first half of the Great Tribulation, leaving 1,335 days for Christians to survive without abandoning their faith in Christ. The idea that the sacrifices are stopped when the abomination of desolation enters the Temple, puts Matthew 24 and Daniel 12:11 on the same time line. The Feast of Trumpets will likely occur near the last day of the 1,335 days.

"And brother will deliver brother to death, and father *his* child; and children will rise up against parents and have them put to death. 13 "And you will be hated by all on account of My name, but <u>the one who endures to the end, he shall be saved."</u> (Mark 13:12–13, NASB, EM).

"But you will be delivered up even by parents and brothers and relatives and friends, and they will put *some* of you to death." (Luke 21:16, NASB).

As those in Daniel 12:12 are called blessed when they make it to the 1,335 days without denying Christ, Mark 13:13, which mentions those who endure, must be talking about the same people.

"Because you have kept the word of My perseverance, I also will keep you from the hour of testing, that *hour* which is about to come upon the whole world, to test those who dwell upon the earth." (Revelation 3:10 NASB)

"For God has **not destined us for wrath**, but for obtaining salvation through our Lord Jesus Christ." (1 Thess. 5:9, NASB, EM).

"Much more then, having now been justified by His blood, we shall be **saved from** the **wrath** of God through Him." (Rom. 5:9, NASB). "For the Lord Himself will descend from heaven with a shout, with the voice of the archangel, and with the trumpet of God; and the dead in Christ will **rise first.** 17 Then we who are alive and remain shall be **caught up** together with them in the clouds to meet the Lord in the air, and thus we shall always be with the Lord." (1 Thess. 4:16–17, NASB, EM).

2 Corinthians 12:2, 4: "… such a man was caught up to the third heaven. … 4 was caught up into Paradise, …"(NASB).

"…and you will be gathered up one by one, O sons of Israel. 13 It will come about also in that day that a great trumpet will be blown; …" (Isa. 27:12–13, NASB).

"And then they will see THE SON OF MAN COMING IN CLOUDS with great power and glory." (Mark 13:26 NASB)

"Your dead will live; their corpses will rise. You who lie in the dust, awake and shout for joy, for your dew is as the dew of the dawn, and the earth will give birth to the departed spirits." (Isa. 26:19) "And what I say to you I say to all, 'Be on the alert!'" (Mark 13:37).

"For just as the lightning comes from the east, and flashes even to the west, so shall the coming of the Son of Man be. 28 "Wherever the corpse is, there the vultures will gather." (Matt. 24:27, 28, NASB).

As vultures find a corpse, so the angels join in the rapture of Christians.

"**…AND THE STARS WILL FALL from the sky**, and the powers of the heavens will be shaken. [the wrath of God, fire and brimstone]. 30 and then the sign of the Son of Man will appear in the sky, and then all the **tribes of the earth will mourn**, and **they will see the Son OF Man** COMING ON THE CLOUDS OF THE SKY with power and great glory. 31 "And He will send forth His **angles** with A GREAT TRUMPET and THEY

WILL **GATHER** TOGETHER **HIS elect** from the four winds, from one end of the sky to the other." (Matt.24:29-31, NASB, EM).

In Luke 17:26–29, Jesus says that the last days will be like the days of Noah and Lot. In Genesis 7:4, God says it is going to start raining in four days. In 7:7, Noah and his family enter the ark due to the flood waters. In 7:13, the text says this was on the same day. In 7:16, Noah and his family enter the ark and the Lord closes the door behind them. It seems clear that on the same day the flood came, Noah and his family were saved.

In Genesis 19:1–3, two angels are taken into Lot's house in the evening. In verse 15, morning had dawned and the angels keep telling Lot to get his family to the mountains. Finally in verse 23, Lot arrives in Zoar as the sun rises. Then the fire and brimstone come down.

In both cases, Noah and Lot were saved on the same day that God's wrath came. In Luke, God says it will be the same as it was in the days of Noah and Lot. Therefore the rapture will surely come on the same day as God's wrath begins.

"For the wrath of God is revealed from heaven against all ungodliness and unrighteousness of men, who suppress the truth in unrighteousness," (Rom.1:18, NASB).

"Now the earth was corrupt in the sight of God, and the earth was filled with violence. ... 13 Then God said to Noah, "The end of all flesh has come before Me; for the earth is filled with violence because of them; and behold, I am about to destroy them with the earth." (Gen. 6:11, 13, NASB).

"And the Lord said, "The outcry of Sodom and Gomorrah is indeed great, and their sin is exceedingly grave. ... 32 Then he said, "Oh may the Lord not be angry, and I shall speak only this once; suppose ten are found there?" [Lot is speaking of ten who were not filled with sin and believed in God.] "And He said, "I will not destroy *it* on account of the ten." (Gen. 18:20, 32, NASB).

The Lord poured out fire and brimstone due to disobedience.

"but on the day that Lot went out from Sodom it rained fire and brimstone from heaven and destroyed them all. 30 "It will be just the same on the day that the Son of Man is revealed." (Luke 17:29–30, NASB).

Based on this passage the rapture will occur on the same day God delivers wrath.

At the point that the stars fall from the sky. Revelation 6:13–17 explains that the last half of the Great Tribulation has started. Revelation 7 takes us from earth to heaven to tell us what has already happened in heaven, as the rapture occurred not long before. Revelation 7:4–8 tells of Messianic Jews—Jews who believe in Christ and who are be marked to protect them from wrath.

"And one of the elders answered, saying to me, "These who are clothed in white robes, who are they, and from where have they come?" 14 And I said to him, "My lord, you know." And he said to me, "**These are the ones who come out of the great tribulation**, and they have washed their robes and made them white in the blood of the Lamb." (Rev. 7:13–14, NASB, EM).

"For behold, the Lord is about to come out from His place to punish the inhabitants of the earth for their iniquity; and the earth will reveal her bloodshed, and no longer cover her slain." (Isa. 26:21, NASB).

"In that day the Lord will punish Leviathan the fleeing serpent, with His fierce and great and mighty sword, even Leviathan the twisted serpent; and He will kill the dragon who lives in the sea." (Isa. 27:1, NASB).

In Revelation 20:1–2, 10, and 14–15, Leviathan, the dragon, and the fleeing serpent all refer to Satan.

"AND THE STARS WILL BE FALLING from heaven, and the powers that are in the heavens will be shaken. 26 "And then they will see THE Son of Man COMING IN CLOUDS with great power and glory. 27 "And then He will send forth the angels, and will gather together His elect from the four winds, from the farthest end of the earth, to the farthest end of heaven." (Mark 13:25–27, NASB, EM).

"and the **stars of the sky fell** to the earth, as a fig tree casts its unripe figs when shaken by a great wind. 14 And the sky was split apart like a scroll when it is rolled up; and every mountain and island were moved out of their places. 15 And the kings of the earth and the great men and the commanders and the rich and the strong and every slave and free man, hid themselves in the caves and among the rocks of the mountains; 16 and **they said to the mountains and to the rocks, "Fall on us and hide us from the presence of Him who sits on the throne, and from the <u>wrath</u> of the Lamb; 17 for the <u>great day</u> of their <u>wrath </u>has come; and who is able to stand?**" (Rev. 6:13-17,NASB, EM).

The stars, God's wrath of fire and brimstone, rain down, and the people mourn as in Matthew 24:30.

"After this I saw four angels standing at the four corners of the earth, holding back the four winds of the earth, so that no wind should blow on the earth or on the sea or on any tree." (Rev. 7:1 NASB) "And when He broke the **seventh seal**, there was silence in heaven for about half an hour." (Rev. 8:1, NASB, EM).

These two events of the wind which stops blowing and the "silence in heaven for about half an hour" may be the same time period of half an hour. This may be saying that the rapture occurs, then the wind stops for a half an hour and then God's wrath is poured out. Whether a half hour or a split second both are a short amount of time to occur between rapture and wrath.

In Rev. 8:1 another seal has been opened, signaling a different event has started, God's wrath. Revelation 6:13–17 spent just enough time to let us know that the last half of the Great Tribulation started with the stars falling form the sky. Now in verse 1 of Revelation 8, the text picks up on the wrath with which Revelation 6:13–17 left off, telling us about all the wrath that those who did not accept Christ are going to suffer.

Thinking about the Probability

In Matthew 24:15, Jesus calls Daniel a prophet. As was discussed in chapter 5, "Coming of Age: The 'Last Days' Overall Time Period," Daniel describes the time as the latter part of the Industrial Age—"many shall run to and fro"—and the Information Age—"and knowledge shall be increased …" (KJV).

To be a reliable prophet, Daniel had to describe the last half of the Industrial Age accurately and describe the Information Age accurately. No age could come between these two ages, and no new age could come into full swing until the "things" Jesus mentioned came to pass. To make this prophecy by logic and imagination would be very difficult to do, so long ago.

Jesus also lays out a time period, which to be true prophecy, must come within the time period, or be the same time period Daniel mentioned and must start with the unlikely event of Israel being reborn as a nation. In addition, Israel must be reborn suddenly, in one day (Isa. 66:8). False Christs, wars, rumors of war, and famines must occur and increase during the time period Christ mentions. There must be a large number of Christians martyred during this time period. There must be a very rare set of four blood moons that occur near the end of the generation Jesus mentions, with accompanying solar eclipses. Lawlessness then must increase.

It is very unlikely that all of these events would occur by chance to fulfill a prophecy. Is this simply looking for "things" that are occurring and using them to fill in the blanks? There have been too many specific events, such as Israel being reborn, born in one day, to fit a mental mind-set of "find an event and force it to fit."

Now lawlessness must increase. "The" Temple must be rebuilt in Jerusalem Israel. Israel must sign a seven year peace treaty. The sacrifices must be started again in the Temple. The sacrifices must then be carried out for three and a half years according to the Jewish calendar. Then the abomination of desolation must desecrate the Temple, at which time the Great Tribulation starts. Which will add to the improbability.

21   To Those Who Believe There Is No God

We all think our perception of reality is correct. Whose reality is reality?

Stephen Hawking has said:

"There is fossil evidence, that there was some form of life on earth, about three and a half billion years ago. This may have been only 500 million years after the earth became stable and cool enough, for life to develop. But life could have taken 7 billion years to develop, and still have left time to evolve to beings like us, who could ask about the origin of life. If the probability of life developing on a given planet, is very small, why did it happen on earth, in about one 14th of the time available".

Hawking admits, "We do not know how DNA molecules first appeared" (www.hawking.org.uk/life-in-the-universe.html). 3/28/2016

Richard Dawkins and Ben Stein have discussed how life began:

> Richard Dawkins: "Well … it could come about in the following way: it could be that what uh at some earlier time somewhere in the universe a civilization e-evolved … by probably some kind of Darwinian means to a very, very high level of technology and designed a form of life that they seeded … perhaps … this planet. Um now that is a possibility."
>
> Dawkins: "We know the sort of event that must have happened for the origin of life."
>
> Ben Stein : "And what was that?"
>
> Dawkins: "It was the origin of the first replicating molecule."

Stein: "Right, and how did that happen?"

Dawkins: "I've told you, we don't know."

Stein: "So you have no idea how it started?"

Dawkins: "No, no, Nor has anyone."

(www.imdb. com/title/tt1091617/quotes) 3/28/2016

To hear more from Ben Stein, you might want to read his book, *"Expelled": No Intelligence Allowed* by Ben Stein

Stephen Hawkins and Richard Dawkins are extremely intelligent. Most of us do not have the IQs or knowledge close to what they have. Their statements give us more to think about.

Since the late 1960s or early 1970s, many of us have been told that life started in a primordial soup. Perhaps this was in a warm ocean tidal pool, near smokers (volcanic vents on the floor of the ocean), or even in ice.

About that time, or even in the 1980s, anyone who suggested that aliens had created life on earth would have been laughed off the planet by most scientists. We live on a planet ideally suited for life. Why then move away from the idea that life started on earth?

Why are many of the world's greatest minds moving to the point of view that we don't know how life started, or that life might even have started on another planet? This more recent view postulates that life started in a primordial soup; eventually life was perhaps living in rock on that planet. Then this location was perhaps struck by an asteroid, which carried that life to earth. This is the Lithopanspermia theory, not the theory Richard Dawkins nor Stephen Hawking mentioned.

One of the following two concepts is likely what Richard Dawkins was considering. Life began on another planet, evolved to a greater mental and technological degree than we have, and then sent "seeds" of life out into space, to plant life on other planets. A second twist is that aliens evolved to such a high degree that they traveled to other planets and seeded life themselves. These examples would be *directed panspermia*, intentional seeding.

Consider life starting on Mars, one of the closest planets to earth and therefore one of the most likely to seed life on earth. Mars for the most part is frozen, one to three miles deep. Being a bit smaller than earth, Mars has less gravitational pull, making it unable to hold lighter gases, nor much of the heavier gases. Therefore, its atmosphere is approximately one one-hundredth that of earth. Mars has very little oxygen and little or no ozone layer.

Very little ozone means the Martian surface has almost no protection from the sun's UV and UB rays, which are responsible for some skin cancers and some macular degeneration. There is no magnetosphere like the earth's Van Allen belt—no magnetic core in Mars to protect life from dangerous solar radiation that can kill.

Had life started and been seeded from another planet outside of our galaxy by Lithopanspermia, it would experience interstellar winds in transit, receiving even greater doses of radiation.

About the only natural method of transportation for microorganisms would be a rocky environment jettisoned into space by an asteroid. Such an asteroid would likely be traveling thousands of miles per hour. It would come crashing down to Mars, striking that planet's surface and launching rock into space.

Astronauts experience a slowly increasing acceleration into space. Now think of sitting in your car on a railroad track and being hit by a freight train running at full speed. Would you live? Perhaps. However, the freight train would not launch you into space. It would require a much stronger impact to launch material into space. Would the microorganism live through the sudden G force, or be ripped apart being thrown across a rough interior surface of the rock? It should have a seat belt.

In space it is cold, near absolute zero, approximately –454 degrees Fahrenheit. The exact temperature is not that important. What is important is how this might affect the microorganism: think of the pasteurization of milk. "The UK Dairy Products Hygiene Regulations 1995 require that milk be treated for 15 seconds at 71.7 degrees centigrade." Found on Wikipedia (https://en.wikipedia.org/wiki/Pasteurization) 3/28/2016.

This flash process kills the bacteria. In the example we are talking about, a micro-organism which would go from cold, warm up while being launched into space, go to near absolute zero and then rapidly get very hot when entering earth's atmosphere.

This microbe would need to be within rock that is well sealed. Otherwise the vacuum of space might rip kill it. It is unlikely that the rock that surrounded this life would be thick enough to protect it from the sun's radiation. In that case, most microorganisms would most likely die, as some of this radiation is the same type of radiation that is released when a nuclear weapon explodes. If this micro-organism were not encased in rock it might have a slower and cooler entry in earth's atmosphere, yet would then receive even more exposure to solar radiation and the vacuum of space.

Scientists may find microorganisms which have survived the vacuum of space, freezing, and solar radiation for a few years. However just as people get skin cancer after years of exposure to sun light, even hardy microorganisms which are exposed to interstellar radiation in galaxies over years, will very likely expire due to the great dosage of radiation.

This rock taxicab, with its tiny passenger microbes, is flying through space—but to where? The trajectory, the precise direction of travel, must be nearly perfect for it to arrive on earth. That's very unlikely even from nearby Mars, and much, much more unlikely to have occurred from another galaxy, even with a massive seeding.

Sadly, even though scientists with great minds spend much time to guarantee the safe reentry of our astronauts, on one occasion the tiles on a shuttle were damaged, resulting in great heat. This resulted in great loss—loss of life. Sometimes no matter how much we think, we cannot think of every possibility.

Before entering earth's atmosphere, spacecraft are slowed down for the crew's safety. A rock approaching earth will only speed up, due to the pull of the earth's gravity. Many of you have seen a falling star or have seen the video of a meteor that fell over Russia in the not-too-distant past. These meteors are burning and may rip apart in a fiery blast.

The rock carrying this small package of life is going to heat up fast. If the rock is large enough, it might protect its contents from the heat. The more porous the meteor's surface, the more friction there is apt to be, thereby increasing heat—unless, of course, the surface were to be magically aerodynamic, like a golf ball designed to be aerodynamic, which might reduce friction a bit. If the rock is strong enough to take the reentry jolt and the correct reentry angle occurs by chance, the microorganism might live. If any of these circumstances are not just right, the micro traveler is toast.

Then this rock as a spacecraft softly lands … No, it doesn't. It smashes into the earth or the ocean. This rock carrying life has gone from near -454 degrees Fahrenheit to possibly burning up in a very short time. If the rock heats up like a Roman candle, then cools quickly in the ocean, it could be a great pasteurization process, leading to death for the microorganism.

Welcome to earth. If this very, very small life form survives all of this, it needs to land in an environment in which it can survive. It needs the correct amount of sunlight or none, liquid that is not too acidic or too corrosive, and so on. Everything must be just right, just by chance.

This description is a general idea of some of the problems involving Lithopanspermia—life seeded to earth by chance. If these microorganisms lived through space travel and somehow broke free from a meteor or asteroid, their light weight might give them a better chance of making earth's surface alive.

However, don't trust the source of this writing. Consult several authorities who have higher education in science and compare their answers on each point. There are many opinions. Scientists have found nucleobases, the chemical building blocks necessary for DNA and RNA, in meteorites. Information found on Earth Sky (earthsky.org/space/earthly-life-arose-from,space-materials-scientists-say) 3/28/2016 This is intriguing evidence, yet not proof of panspermia.

Those who believe directed panspermia seeded life on earth avoid some of the problems of Lithopanspermia. Directed panspermia requires a habitable planet, perhaps like earth, where life could have evolved by chance, though very intelligent scientists don't know how that would occur. Before their star burned out or went supernova, before the inhabitants destroyed their planet's environment, before they were thrown out of a habitable orbit by another planet, before nuclear weapons destroyed them, before a large asteroid or rogue planet wiped them out—before any of this could happen, they must have become far more technologically advanced than the inhabitants of earth are now, and able to seed life into space to some effective degree.

This concept relies on the thought that there are other, perhaps many, habitable planets in our universe. Life needs a star with a long, stable life. The typical-sized white dwarf stars (our sun is somewhat larger than the typical dwarf) will not go supernova, which would extinguish life on its orbiting planets. Stars that do not eventually go supernova do not seed planetary material. Dwarf stars account for perhaps 80 to 90 percent of stars in our known universe but have a more narrow habitable zone.

We are living in the Milky Way Galaxy, with enough red giant stars available to produce planetary material when they go supernova—a quantity of red giants most galaxies do not have. Supernova explosions that produced planetary material in the very distant past should be considered as adding to the amount of planetary material.

What percentage of solar systems have a warm, fairly stable, long-burning star like our sun; have a planet that resides within a narrow habitable zone; with a heavy metal core producing heat; spin that is a part of generating a magnetosphere; have volcanic vents that produce movement in the core;

have a crust thick enough to protect its inhabitants and insulate the core to maintain heat, yet also allows for subduction zones, the subduction zones helping create the possibility of a CO_2 recycling system; has a moon large enough to stabilize wobble, a moon that is not slowly falling into its planet; have in its neighborhood a large Jupiter-type planet whose gravity pulls in numerous asteroids, thereby decreasing the number of asteroids that could hit their planet; is far enough from stars poised to go supernova; is not in its galaxy's core where there is a great amount of radiation; is far from magna stars? And these factors are far from the number of cosmological fine-tuning factors, nor among the more improbable required for life as we know it.

There are many stars and many planets, giving many possibilities. True. In fact astronomers occasionally mention that they have found an earthlike planet. However, do such planets have all the mentioned factors, or even most of them? Considering all the factors needed for a habitable planet, then reducing by probability for each factor, the likelihood of a planet that will support life similar to ourselves drops rapidly. Are there extremophiles out there? Consider the probability of the simplest single organism forming by chance.

The directed panspermia theory has its problems. Despite those problems, some very intelligent scientists seem to be currently favoring it as the best explanation for life on earth. This would mean that on that distant planet, that first replicating cell formed by chance, by means that are still unknown, and rose to great intelligence, and greater capabilities than our civilization. Then directed panspermia could occur.

Currently there is no scientific proof of the first self-replicating cell forming by chance and no scientific proof that directed panspermia or Lithopanspermia have occurred. To believe self-replicating life formed by chance, in some kind of primordial soup, on another planet is to believe, <u>by faith</u>, that evolution occurred there and these aliens were then able to seed life. Again, currently there is no scientific proof.

Despite my lack of confidence in the theory of panspermia, It would not be surprising to soon hear scientists say they have found a planet that is thought to have all the necessary qualities, more likely habitable than ones found to date. Things are not always as they appear. One of the most recent earthlike planets (Kepler-452b's) discovered is approximately 60 percent larger than earth. Its gravity would then also be approximately 60 percent greater. Someone on earth weighing 100 pounds would feel like they weighed about 160 pounds on said planet, and someone weighing 200 pounds on earth would feel like they weighed about 320 pounds on that planet. This would create great stress on bones, joints and structural tissues. This does not mean there could not be life there, it just points out a potential problem. (www.cnn.com/2015/07/23/us/feat-nasa-kepler-planetdiscovery/) 3/28/2016

Suppose there were one or more planets as habitable as earth. Then there is still another problem to overcome. In Stephen Meyer's book *Signature in the Cell* (New York: HarperOne, 2009), Meyer mentions a calculation which has been calculated by more than one scientist (you can find this on pages 210–213). They calculate the probability of amino acids lining up to create a functional protein, the correct protein. Then approximately 249 more functional proteins, the correct proteins needed, must be produced by chance. Then these proteins must join correctly just to produce a simple modest functional cell.

This is an oversimplification, but the problem is that this probability is estimated to be approximately 1 in 10 to the $40,000^{th}$ power. Compare this to the estimated number of electrons, protons, and neutrons in the known universe, approximately 10 to the 80th power. These odds are so high that most of us have nothing to compare to for understanding. If 10 to the $40,000^{th}$ power is reasonably possible, then it should be very, very, very easy to win the Power Ball jackpot at one in 292,201,338 (3/2016) or rounded up to approximately 30 to the 7th power.

There are numerous other known, highly improbable factors as stated in *The Creator and the Cosmos.*

The most improbable may be human DNA, as Dr. Sanford talks about our DNA being "poly-functional" with high information density (p. 133) in *Genetic Entropy & The Myster of the Genome*. For our DNA to occur by evolutionary chance, our DNA would have had to first go through the first steps of becoming a simple single cell organism and also evolving.

Scientists observing the formation of galaxies arrived at the conclusion that star mass alone does not seem to adequately explain how galaxies form and hold together. This requires more gravity, requiring more mass. This was the beginning of the concept of *dark matter.*

The clumping of matter to produce habitable galaxies must be somewhat precise. Dark matter is unseen, unfelt, and apparently only interacts with our known universe through gravity. The mathematical models have estimated that this dark matter makes up almost 75 to 90 percent of our universe's matter, perhaps more. To believe that dark matter exists is to believe in it due to its effect. Currently dark matter cannot be proven to exist by sight, touch, hearing, or scientific experiment—only that something is having a gravitational effect.

The fact that dark matter seems to have such an important effect on our universe, and in addition that its effect must be so precise, might lead some to conclude that there might be intelligence directing the existence and behavior of dark matter.

Stephen Hawking stated, "God was not needed to create the universe. The Big Bang was the result of the inevitable laws of physics and did not need God to spark the creation of the universe"(www.telegraph.co.uk/news/ science/science/-news/7976594/Stephen-Hawking-God-was-not-needed-to-create-the-Universe.html 3/28/2016

Stephen Hawking is incredibly intelligent, making it difficult to disagree with him. If, however, God created the laws of physics (etc.), then yes, there would be an essential need for God.

There is no point in arguing the issue, as either point of view might give evidence. However, neither point of view has been absolutely proven by scientific experiment, at least not to date.

The intent is not to attack science, as science is great. The point is for us to truthfully ask, has science come to the point that there is scientific proof—not theory, but observation and experimentation—that there is no God? Is there proof as to how life came to be?

Perhaps the fact that it is possible to solve problems using physics, and those laws keep working, has become so compelling that it is difficult for some people to seriously consider God. The fact that someone does not find God necessary does not, of course, prove God is nonexistent.

Dark matter is thought to be found throughout the universe, even passing though us without our ever being aware of it. Like dark matter's estimated percentage of mass in the universe, so too, God fills the heavens. "Am I a God who is near," declares the Lord, "and not a God far off? 24 … "Do I not fill the heavens and the earth?" declares the Lord." (Jeremiah 23:23, 24, NASB).

Some contemporary scientists think there is evidence of higher dimensions, which could be very close to us. In addition, if there were beings (or God) living in one of these dimensions, they might be able to see us, yet we would not see them.

"Oh, that Thou wouldst rend the heavens and come down, … (Isa. 64:1, NASB).

"And the sky was split apart like a scroll when it is rolled up; …" (Rev. 6:14, NASB).

"And He said to him, "Truly, truly, I say to you, you shall see the heavens opened, and the angels of God ascending and descending on the Son of Man." (John 1:51, NASB).

Could it be that, rather than aliens or a precise balance of dark matter by chance, that it is God who is hidden from us, as though behind a curtain to be pulled back?

Those of us who believe there is a God seem to have something in common with brilliant minds like Stephen Hawking and Richard Dawkins, who do not believe there is a God. These brilliant minds seem to believe—have faith—that the first self-replicating life occurred by chance. Neither they, nor those of us who believe there is a God can prove our beliefs. Yet those who believe there is a God, and those who do not, have confidence, belief, in something that cannot absolutely be proven.

It will be interesting to see what the next fifteen years hold. Hopefully it will not be like the old Chinese curse: "May you live in interesting times."

> Jesus "For what does it profit a man to gain the whole world, and forfeit his soul?" (Mark 8:36, NASB).

> Jim Elliot: "He is no fool who gives what he cannot keep to gain that which he cannot lose." (www2.wheaton.edu/bgc/archives/faq/20.htm) 3/28/2016

Blaise Pascal was a genius mathematician and physicist. He said, in the *Pensées*:

> "God is, or He is not." But to which side shall we incline? Reason can decide nothing here. There is an infinite chaos which separated us. A game is being played at the extremity of this infinite distance where heads or tails will turn up. What will you wager? According to reason, you can neither the one thing nor the other, according to reason, you can defend neither of the propositions.

> Do not, then, reprove for the error those who have made a choice; for again you know nothing about it. "No, but I blame them for having made, not this choice, but a choice; for again both he who chooses tails are equally at

fault, they are both in the wrong. The true course is not to wager at all."

"That is very fine. Yes, I must wager; but I may perhaps wager too much." Let us see. Since there is an equal risk of gain and of loss, if you had only to gain two lives, instead of one, you might still wager. But if there were three lives to gain, you would have to play (since you are under the necessity of playing), and you would be imprudent, when you are forced to play, not to chance your life to gain three at a game where there is an equal risk of loss and gain. But there is an eternity of life and happiness. And this being so, if there were an infinity of chances, of which only one would be for you, you would still be right in wagering one to win two, and you would act stupidly, being obliged to play, by refusing to stake one life against three at a game in which out of an infinity of chances there is one for you, if there were an infinity of an infinity of a happy life to gain. But there is here an infinity of and infinity happy life to gain, a chance of gain against a finite number of chances of loss, and what you stake is finite." (http.//en.wikipedia. org/wiki/Pascal%27s_Wager) 3/28/2016

You may wager that there is no God. Your profit—you can choose to do anything you wish. Your potential loss—if the God of the Bible is reality, you lose eternal life in heaven, with the certainty of eternal separation from God, should God exist.

You wager that the God of the Bible does exist and accept Christ. Your potential profit—eternity in heaven with God, and on earth you can still enjoy friends, family, and so on. Your loss—you must pursue obeying God, which does not allow you to do anything you wish, and if your wager is wrong, there is no gain of eternal life.

Pascal is stating that you must wager. If you claim not to wager, you will have wagered by not having accepted Christ as God and Savior. This is choice by default, as in tennis when the ball is not served into the in play area. Is the potential temporary gain worth the potential eternal loss?

For decades we were told life began in a primordial soup of some kind. Now it is suggested life was seeded from another planet, without scientific proof. If you can't prove by experiment how life began, if you have equations but cannot absolutely prove by experiment what happened and what was before the Big Bang, your risk may be higher than you have calculated.

If you already believed in something that has not been proven scientifically such as life evolving on earth, and the most acceptable theory keeps changing, how unreasonable is it to believe in God, who has not been proven by scientific experiment either?

It might be wise to consider reading the suggested books and Jesus's teachings in the New Testament before making a final decision. I encourage you not to judge quickly based on what others think. Eternity is a long time. If Israel starts rebuilding the temple soon, you might want to think even harder and with a greater sense of urgency.

There is no need to have concern about a God who does not exist. Would a human have written the following, approximately twenty five hundred years ago. "… Was I not silent even for a long time so you do not fear Me?" (Isaiah 57:11, NASB).

From Joshua 24:15 "…choose for yourselves today whom you will serve:… "(NASB) God has given us the free will to choose (Deut. 30:19&20 also) I encourage you to serve Christ. There are some people who believe that predestination, which is mentioned in Romans 8:30 and Ephesians 5:1, means we have no ability to choose. God, knowing all things, knew the decisions each of us would make from the moment He chose to create us, and in that way God did predestine us. However, as Joshua 24:15 and Deuteronomy 30 state, God gives the free will to choose. God's foreknowledge does not mean we do not have the free will to choose. It simply means God already knows our choices. I am not aware of any mention of any town or any contact with other people in hell, just suffering. An eternity of heaven or hell is in your hands.

22   God Plans a Relationship with Mankind

Suppose there was a God, an almighty, all-knowing, all-wise, all-just, all-loving God, and nothing else existed. "I am the Lord, and there is no other; Besides Me there is no God. ..." (Isa. 45:5, NASB). Perhaps this God would consider these qualities to be wasted without purpose, without something or someone to enjoy these attributes. So perhaps this God would decide to create human beings. These creatures of His should appreciate the gift of life and relationships with other human beings, giving thanks to their Creator. Does the Bible say this is what God thought? No, this is conjecture.

To create a mindless robot or a brain-dead zombie slave would be pointless, like having a conversation with a recorded message. Such a creature would need to be self-aware, but most of all have free will—to do as it pleases. Free will, so that a show of appreciation would be from the heart. With free will, many would fake a loving relationship to please their Creator, yet seek their own will. With free will, some or many would openly rebel against their Creator and the sound reason of love and respect. They might also treat each other with disrespect and evil acts. These actions would nullify the very purpose of creating these beings.

God says in Leviticus 11:45, "...you shall be holy for I am holy." (NASB). The standard must be high, so that heaven, real life, will be a wonderful place to live and that God will be respected

"But I say to you that everyone who is angry with his brother shall be guilty before the court; and whoever shall say to his brother, Raca,' [meaning empty-headed] shall be guilty before the supreme court; and whoever shall say, 'You fool,' shall be guilty *enough* to go into the fiery hell." (Matt. 5:22, NASB).

"You have heard that it was said, 'You shall not commit adultery'; 28 but I say to you, that everyone who looks on a woman to lust for her has committed adultery with her in his heart." (Matt. 5:27-28, NASB).

"And his lord, moved with anger, handed him over to the torturers until he should repay all that was owed him. 35 "So shall My heavenly Father also do to you, if each of you does not forgive his brother from your heart." (Matt. 18:34–35, NASB).

"for all have sinned and fall short of the glory of God," (Rom. 3:23, NASB).

"If we say that we have no sin, we are deceiving ourselves, and the truth is not in us." (1 John1:8, NASB).

My creatures need to respect Me and desire to be holy of their own free will. On the other hand, how would My creatures, My people, know good if they do not know evil? It is not My desire to condemn those who are to be my people—those who have free will and seek Me—unless first giving them opportunity to repent. With free will, people will understand good and evil.

"So give Thy servant an understanding heart to judge Thy people to discern between good and evil. For who is able to judge this great people of thine?" (1 Kings 3:9, NASB).

If I allow My creation to see Me, some will only lie and deceive, attempting to hide their contempt for Me. It is not in Me to allow evil to reign. Justice is required. Those who are hateful and disrespectful, creating contention, would destroy My plan for love and respect and showing contempt for their creator.

"He presented another parable to them, saying. "The kingdom of heaven may be compared to a man who sowed good seed in his field. 25 "But while men were sleeping, his enemy came and sowed tares also among the wheat, and went away. 26 "But when the wheat sprang up and bore grain, then the tares became evident also. 27 "And the slaves of the landowner came and said to him, 'Sir, did you not sow good seed in your field? How then does it have tares?' 28 "And he said to them, 'An enemy has done this!' And the slaves said to him, 'Do you want us, then, to go and gather them up?' 29 "But he said, 'No; lest while you are gathering up the tares, you may root up the wheat with them. 30 'Allow both to grow together until the harvest; and in the time of the harvest I will say to the reapers, "First gather up the tares and bind them in bundles to burn them up; but gather the wheat into my barn."'" (Matt. 13:24–30, NASB).

"Then He left the multitudes, and went into the house. And His disciples came to Him, saying, "Explain to us the parable of the tares of the field." 37 And He answered and said, "The one who sows the good seed is the Son of Man, 38 and the field is the world; and as for the good seed, these are the sons of the kingdom; and the tares are the sons of the evil one; 39 and the enemy who sowed them is the devil, and the harvest is the end of the age; and the reapers are angels. 40 "Therefore just as the tares are gathered up and burned with fire, so shall it be at the **end of the age.**" (Matt. 13:36–40, NASB, EM).

By allowing life together, all understanding good and evil, God gives everyone the opportunity to follow Him.

Isn't it our life? Shouldn't we be allowed to do as we please? Is this life we seem to live even life, or is it actually more similar to a class with a decision to make and real life comes later?

"Woe to the *one* who quarrels with his Maker—an earthenware vessel among the vessels of earth! Will the clay say to the potter, 'What are you doing?' Or the thing you are making say, 'He has no hands?'" (Isa. 45:9, NASB). If we are created beings, don't we owe everything that we have and everything we are to God? Those who were born with exceptional musical talent and athletes born with athletic skill may work hard to achieve their success, yet all talents were given, such as skill and the ability to work hard. Shouldn't the created respect its Creator?

What is done with a car when it is no longer drivable? It ends up in the junkyard. Should we expect anything less than God's judgment? After all, almost all of the commands for us to follow were also intended for others, that we might be treated well also.

"Now there was a certain rich man, and he habitually dressed in purple and fine linen, gaily living in splendor every day. 20 "And a certain poor man named Lazarus was laid at his gate, covered in sores, 21 and longing to be fed with the *crumbs* which were falling from the rich man's table; besides, even the dogs were coming and licking his sores. 22 "Now it came about that the poor man died and he was carried away by the angels to Abraham's bosom; and the rich man also died and was buried. 23 "And in Hades he lifted up his eyes, being in torment, and saw Abraham far away, and Lazarus in his bosom. 24 "And he cried out and said, 'Father Abraham, have mercy on me, and send Lazarus, that he may dip the tip of his finger in water and cool off my tongue; for I am in agony in this flame.' 25 "But Abraham said, 'Child, remember that during your life you received good things, and likewise Lazarus bad things; but now he is being comforted here, and you are in agony, 26 'And besides all this, between us and you there is a great chasm fixed, in order that those who wish to come over from here to you may not be able, and that none may cross over from there to us." (Luke 16:19–26, NASB).

"No man can by any means redeem his brother, or give to God a ransom for him— 8 For the redemption of his soul is costly, and he should cease trying forever--" (Psalm 49:7–8, NASB).

Yet punishment is not what God desires for anyone. "Thus it is not the will of your Father who is in heaven that one of these little ones perish." (Matt. 18:14, NASB). To what degree is God willing to go to avoid this fate—our separation from God?

"Sing for joy and be glad, O daughter of Zion; for behold I am coming and **I will dwell in your midst," declares the Lord**." (Zech. 2:10, NASB, EM).

"BEHOLD, THE VIRGIN SHALL BE WITH CHILD, AND SHALL BEAR A SON, AND THEY SHALL CALL HIS NAME IMMANUEL," which translated means, "GOD WITH US." (Matt. 1:23, NASB).

"Then Moses said to God, "Behold, I am going to the sons of Israel, and I shall say to them, 'The God of your fathers has sent me to you.' Now they may say to me, 'What is His name?' What shall I say to them?" 14 And God said to Moses, "I AM WHO I AM"; and He said, "Thus you shall say to the sons of Israel, 'I AM has sent me to you...'" 15 ... 'This is My name forever, and **this is My memorial- name to all generations.'"** (Exod. 3:13-15, NASB, EM).

The sons of Israel had not heard from God for approximately four hundred years. Generations had been likely been told, "My father said that his father said that his father said that they heard from God," and the last generation likely thought, "Yeah, right." The word "memorial" speaks of bringing something to mind, in this case God's name.

"I" is first person singular. "Am" is the first person singular verb form of "to be." This name of God is unlike the names humans have given other gods, such as Thor, intended to show power. God's name itself answered the Israelites unspoken question and the question of many today. Is there really a God? And God said, "Yes, My name 'I AM' itself says that I exist."

Jesus said, "I said therefore to you, that you shall die in your sins; for unless you believe that **I am** *He*, you shall die in your sins." (John 8:24, NASB, EM). The word *He* in italics was added for understanding. The word *He* is not in the original document. Jesus claimed the same name "I AM" as God did in Exodus 3:14–15. God said it is His memorial name. *Memorial* means to remember. "Remember this is My name: I AM."

"Jesus said to them, "Truly, truly, I say to you, before Abraham was born, I am." 59 Therefore they picked up stones to throw at Him; but Jesus hid Himself, and went out of the temple." (John 8:58–59, NASB). Again Jesus claimed the name of God as His and claimed to be older than Abraham. The Pharisees understood Jesus was claiming to be God, and picked up stones with the intention of stoning Him to death.

"THOU HAST MADE HIM FOR A LITTLE WHILE LOWER THAN THE ANGELS; ..." (Heb. 2:7, NASB).

"For it was the *Father's* good pleasure for all the fullness to dwell in Him." (Col. 1:19, NASB).

"For in Him all the fullness of Deity dwells in bodily form," (Col. 2:9, NASB).

"…Christ Jesus, 6 who, although He existed in the form of God, did not regard equality with God a thing to be grasped, 7 but emptied Himself, taking the form of a bond-servant, and being made in the likeness of men." (Phil. 2:5–7, NASB).

For the purpose of paying the debt of mankind's sin, Jesus, God in the flesh, did not grasp (that is hold on to) His power as God.

Jesus claims the title "Son of God":

"He who believes in Him is not judged; he who does not believe has been judged already, because he has not believed in the name of only begotten Son of God." (John 3:18, NASB).

"do you say of Him, whom the Father sanctified and sent into the world, 'You are blaspheming,' because I said, 'I am the Son of God'? 37 "If I do not do the works of My Father, do not believe Me; 38 but if I do them, though you do not believe Me, believe the works, that you may know and understand that the Father is in Me, and I in the Father." (John 10:36–38, NASB).

Satan tempted Jesus to use His power, to prove He is the "Son of God." "and said to Him, "If You are the Son of God throw Yourself down; for it is written, 'He WILL GIVE His ANGLES CHARGE CONCERNING You;'" (Matt. 4:6, NASB), Satan desired to provoke Jesus by questioning His title, the "Son of God."

The Pharisees called Jesus a glutton and a drunkard: "The Son of Man has come eating and drinking; and you say, 'Behold, a gluttonous man, and a drunkard, a friend of tax-gatherers and sinners!' 35 "Yet wisdom is vindicated by all her children." (Luke 7:34-35, NASB).

If a beagle had puppies, the puppies would have long floppy ears, four legs, short legs compared to many dogs, and most likely brown, black and white coats, all similar to their mother. If wisdom had children, they would be wise, an inherited attribute, and point out the errors of the Pharisees. If God had a Son, the Son would have the same attributes as God, such as deity—to be God.

"Now that no one is justified by the Law before God is evident; for, "THE RIGHTEOUS MAN SHALL LIVE BY FAITH."" (Gal. 3:11, NASB). No matter what good deeds we have done, we have still broken God's laws, which shows disrespect to God.

"But God demonstrates His own love toward us, in that while we were yet sinners, Christ died for us." (Romans 5:8, NASB).

"Men of Israel, listen to these words; Jesus the Nazarene, a man attested to you by God with miracles and wonders and signs which God performed through Him in your midst, just as you yourselves know— 23 this Man, delivered up by the predetermined plan and foreknowledge of God, you nailed to a cross by the hands of godless men and put Him to death. 24 "And God raised Him up again, putting an end the agony of death, since it was impossible for Him to be held in its power." (Acts 2:22–24, NASB, EM).

"nevertheless knowing that a man is not justified by the works of the Law but through faith in Christ Jesus, even we have believed in Christ Jesus, that we may be justified by faith in Christ, and not by the works of the Law; since by the works of the Law shall no flesh be justified." (Gal. 2:16, NASB).

So apparently before creation, God knew that no one would avoid rebelling—sinning against Him. However, already loving His creation before you and I came into existence, God had a plan. God would live with mankind—live in a human body, keep company with His creation and teach us—and He, Jesus, God in the flesh, would receive the punishment we deserve, the full wrath we deserve. "…He, your Teacher will no longer hide Himself, but your eyes will behold your Teacher." (Isa. 30:20, NASB).

Then Jesus the Son was spit upon by his creation and mocked verbally. A crown of thorns was placed on His head and the thorns driven into His head seemingly with woven reeds. Then they crucified him, driving nails through His hands and feet. Although crucifixion is a painful death, from God's perspective it does not seem to be the most painful punishment.

"Christ redeemed us from the curse of the Law, having become a curse for us—for it is written, "CURSED IS EVERYONE WHO HANGS ON A 'TREE--" (Gal. 3:13, NASB). See also Deut. 21:22–23)

Painful as it must have been to be rejected by His own creation, the worst pain may have been to be made to be sinful, being Himself sinless. He became as though He had committed sin and received the wrath, His wrath, which we deserve, Himself. Christ took the punishment we deserve so that we can have eternal salvation and the joy of living with Him eternally.

"Behold, I stand at the door and knock; if anyone hears My voice and opens the door, I will come in to him, and will dine with him, and he with Me." (Rev. 3:20, NASB). The apostle Paul, who followed the Jewish law very carefully, yet called himself the worst of all sinners likely because he had persecuted and killed the very Christians who were trying to lead him to Christ. Christ accepted Paul when Paul repented and accepted Christ as his only method of salvation.

Judas betrayed Christ in almost certainly the most vile of all sins. You and I, like Paul and Judas, have disobeyed God, as though spitting in God's face. Despite this, Jesus said, "if anyone." If Hitler had repented, or did repent before he died, Christ would forgive him, as you and I.

"He who has the Son has the life; he who does not have the Son of God does not have the life." (1 John 5:12, NASB).

"Jesus said to him, "I am the way, and the truth, and the life; no one comes to the Father, but through Me. 7 "If you had known Me, you would have known My Father also; from now on you know Him, and have seen Him." 8 Phillip said to Him, "Lord, show us the Father, and it is enough for us." 9 Jesus said to him, "Have I been so long with you, and yet you have not come to know Me, Philip? He who has seen Me has seen the Father; how do you say, 'Show us the Father?'" (John 14:6–9, NASB).

"He again fixes a certain day, "Today," saying through David after so long a time just as has been said before, "TODAY IF YOU HEAR HIS VOICE, DO NOT HARDEN YOUR HEARTS." (Heb. 4:7, NASB).

There have been those who have suggested that the idea of God is just a crutch. Consider, for example, someone who is street preaching and is being ridiculed. Did they know at the outset that they would be ridiculed? Almost certainly. God is not going to coddle you; in fact, God will likely allow persecution, so that you may grow and prove your allegiance to Him, perhaps like Job. However, Christ will be with you like a great brother.

Most Christians do seem to have a common feeling of being comforted or encouraged by God. Accepting Christ might be compared to following a path that intersects many paths along the way with no markers to be seen. You have the Bible and the knowledge that Christ is with you to stay on course, even if you hear no voice.

If you are ardent in your disbelief in Christianity, you might try something radical and risky: challenge God for a response. Give God a challenge. For instance, "God if you will make this change, such as the healing of a personal relationship or a disease, I will follow you forever." If God is not there He cannot make the miraculous happen. Be prepared to honor your challenge.

I urge you to request, that Christ to come into your life as Master, God, and Savior. We do not know if today might be the last chance.

Whether you make a commitment today or not, I urge you to start reading the Bible, starting in the book of Matthew, right away. Then read the entire

New Testament again a few times. What you read in the New Testament will help in looking for a church that accurately preaches God's word, a local group of Christians to fellowship with.

A Brief View of Some Events That Occur during the Second Portion of the Great Tribulation

"and the stars of the sky fell to the earth,… 15 And the kings of the earth and the great men and the commanders and the rich and the strong and every slave and every free man, hid themselves in the caves and among the rocks of the mountains; 16 and they said to the mountains and to the rocks, "Fall on us and hide us from the presence of Him who sits on the throne, and from the wrath of the Lamb; 17 for the great day of their wrath has come; and who is able to stand?" (Rev. 6:13, 15–17, NASB).

"And the second angel sounded, and something like a great mountain burning with fire was thrown into the sea; and a third of the sea became blood; 9 and a third of the creatures, which were in the sea and had life, died; and a third of the ships were destroyed. 10 And the third angel sounded, and a great star fell from heaven, burning like a torch, and it fell on a third of the rivers and on the springs of waters; 11 and the name of the star is called Wormwood; and a third of the waters became wormwood; and many men died from the waters, because they were made biter." (Rev. 8:8–11, NASB).

Scientists have found an asteroid, #99942, named Apophis, which has an orbit that makes it one of the most likely asteroids to impact earth. This orbit will bring Apophis back toward earth either in a near miss or an impact on Friday the 13th in April 2029. Jesus' mention of a generation that would see the things He stated, which completes with the rapture, and should end by approximately 2028, at which time the last portion of the Great Tribulation starts. God's wrath, including something like a great mountain thrown into the sea, in Rev. 8:8. Apophis is estimated to weigh approximately 25 million tons, is approximately 820 feet wide, and it is moving at approximately 28,000 miles per hour. It has been estimated that there is only an approximate 3 percent chance that Apophis will strike earth. The timing is interesting. See https://en.wikipedia.org/wiki/99942_Apophis 3/28/2016 and NASA. neo.jpl.nasa.gov/Apophis. 3/28/2016

"And out of the smoke came forth locusts upon the earth; and <u>power was given them</u>, as the scorpions of the earth have power. 4 And they were told that they should not hurt the grass of the earth, nor any green thing, nor any tree, but only the men who do not have the seal of God on their foreheads." (Rev. 9:3–4, NASB, EM).

"A third of mankind was killed by these three plagues, by the fire and the smoke and the brimstone, which proceeded out of their mouths." (Rev. 9:18, NASB).

"And the first angel went and poured out his bowl into the earth; and it became a loathsome and malignant sore upon the men who had the mark of the beast and who worshiped his image." (Rev. 16:2, NASB).

"And the fourth angel poured out his bowl upon the sun; and it was given to it to scorch men with fire. 9 And men were scorched with fierce heat; and they blasphemed the name of God who has the power over these plagues; and they did not repent, so as to give Him glory." (Rev. 16:8–9, NASB).

"…the light of the sun will be seven times *brighter*, like the light of seven days, on the day the Lord binds up the fracture of His people…" (Isaiah 30:26, NASB).

"And inasmuch as it is appointed for men to die once and after this comes judgment," (Heb. 9:27, NASB).

"For if we go on sinning willfully after receiving the knowledge of the truth, there no longer remains a sacrifice for sins, 27 but a certain terrifying expectation of judgment, and THE FURY OF A FIRE WHICH WILL CONSUME THE ADVERSARIES." (Heb. 10:26–27, NASB).

If you have not accepted Jesus Christ as Master, God, and Savior, I again recommend you do so now. Or at least be investigating the matter with great intensity now.

Sounds insane? You won't believe what you can't prove? After many years of being told that life came about from a primordial soup, some of the greatest scientists admit we don't know how life came about. Some are suggesting life was seeded on earth, even with the complexities that entails. Not knowing how the first life began means you would have to believe in evolution without scientific proof. That is faith. How much more difficult is it to believe there is a God?

23 What Is Soon to Come: Why 2027?

There is no mention that the plagues of the four horses and the fifth seal have stopped. We can expect more false Christs, war, famine, pestilence, earthquakes, violence, and martyrdom.

The events of 9/11 came at the end of the Jewish Shemitah. The hit the United States economy took in 2008 came at the end of the Jewish Shemitah.[1] Rabbi Jonathan Cahn's *Isaiah 9:10* DVD explains how these events compare to a terrorist attack that occurred in Israel, as described in Isaiah 9:10. These calamities seem to be harbingers—warnings for America to repent. Instead of repenting, America seems to be rebelling more. Events similar to those in the fall of 2001 and 2008, such as economic woes, may not be far off.

Previous series of blood moons occurring on Jewish High Holy Days were accompanied by important events for Israel. To avoid war, Israel may sign the peace treaty, or out of necessity go to war to avoid annihilation and then sign the peace treaty. Dan. 9:24–26 seems to make it clear that a peace treaty will be signed.

There is a great earthquake associated with the blood moons in Revelation 6:12. This great earthquake is mentioned in the first part of this split verse. Therefore it seemed most likely to occur during the same time period as the four blood moons; however, that was not the case. It may occur very soon or it might be the earthquake mentioned at the time of the rapture in Isaiah 64:3 (timed with the second portion of the split verse) and Revelation 6:14 which mentions mountains being moved (likely a huge earthquake), or it may happen somewhere in between. This is worth mentioning, as it will most likely be one of the worst in centuries or many centuries or even recorded history; otherwise it probably would not be noted as "great."

Regarding the Temple in Jerusalem: the rebuilding of the temple should start soon, and this might be a rapid build (see Dan. 9:25). There must be time to rebuild the Temple and carry out the sacrifices for three and a half years before approximately 2024-2027, if I have understood Jesus's statements correctly. The day the sacrifices start, the countdown starts—from then there are approximately three and a half years until the Great Tribulation. (See Dan. 9:27, 11:31; Matt. 24:25; 2 Thess. 2:1–8.)

The Temple is desecrated.

The Great Tribulation starts when the abomination of desolation desecrates the temple or when he attacks Israel. These likely occur with little time in between.

The Great Tribulation starts.

There will almost certainly be efforts to make it very difficult for Christians to live, to even eke out an existence, an extreme struggle.

More earthquakes will occur, likely large earthquakes.

Matthew 24:8 describes birth pangs; things keep getting worse. Revelation 6:8 describes the ashen horse; terrible events keep getting worse.

Then there will be attempts to lure Christians into false religion and to bait Christians to look for Christ here or there and kill them. There will be more acts of martyrdom, as ISIS has been carrying out (Matt.24:23-27). We can expect to see miraculous wonders performed that may mislead even the elect (Matt. 24:24). Many who now profess Christ are now already being deceived by the lies they are being told.

"…yet they will fall by sword and by flame,…" (Dan. 11:33, NASB). This occurred in the German gas chambers in World War II, during the latter part of the Industrial Age. On 9/11 many were burned to death in the twin towers. This death by "flame" came again as we saw ISIS in the news. CBS 2/4/2015 "Jordanian pilot's obscene burning death by ISIS sparks outrage in Mideast" (www.cbsnews.com/news/jordanian-pilots-obscene-burning-death-by-isis-sp) 3/30/2016 (www.dailymail.co.uk.../PIERS-MORGAN-Watching-ISIS-burn-man-alive) 3/29/2016

CNN "February 19, 2015 "ISIS burned up 40 people alive, official in Iraq says," (www.cnn.com/2015/02/18/mideast/isis-iraq-people-burned). 3/29/2016 UPI 2/19/2015 "Islamic State burns at least 40 people alive" ([www.upi.com/Top News/...burns-at...40-people](www.upi.com/Top_News/...burns-at...40-people)) 3/30/2016

Christians will be martyred and persecuted, likely beyond what they think they can withstand. Continue to rely on Christ. Numerous writers refer to the Great Tribulation period as lasting seven years. This would make the first half approximately three and a half years. Daniel mentions two specific amounts of time. which seem to describe the time to the end of the sacrifices, including the abomination being set up 1,290 days and then the first portion of the Great Tribulation, 1,335 days. "And from the time that the regular sacrifice is abolished, and the abomination of desolation is set up, there will be 1,290 days. 12 "How blessed is he who keeps waiting and attains to the 1,335 days!" (Dan. 12:11–12, NASB).

You may want to consult the teachings of Hal Lindsay, Perry Stone, Pat Robertson, and John Hagee to gain greater insight.

"And he will make a firm covenant with the many for one week, but in the middle of the week he will put a stop to sacrifice and grain offering; and on the wing of abominations will come one who makes desolate, even until a complete destruction, one that is decreed, is poured out on the one who makes desolate." (Dan. 9:27, NASB).

Again if I understand correctly, this will mark the beginning of the Great Tribulation. "Therefore when you see the ABOMINATION OF DESOLATION which was spoken of through Daniel the prophet, standing in the holy place (let the reader understand)" (Matt. 24:15, NASB). At this time the fan turns so brown it won't turn.

"Let no one in any way deceive you, for it will not come unless the apostasy comes first, and the man of lawlessness is revealed, the son of destruction." (2 Thess. 2:3, NASB). Apostasy means falling away from the faith, Christianity.

"Know this first of all, that in the last days mockers will come with their mocking, following after their own lusts, 4 and saying, 'Where is the promise of His coming? For ever since the fathers fell asleep, all continues just as it was from the beginning of creation.'" (2 Pet. 3:3-4, NASB).

"But the Spirit explicitly says that in later times some will fall away from the faith, paying attention to deceitful spirits and doctrines of demons." (1 Tim. 4:1, NASB).

If you recognize these things taking place and at that time have not yet given your life to Christ, realize there is not much time left to commit.

Why 2027?

What would lead to the thought that the Great Tribulation would start by 2027? Jesus mentioned Israel being born or reborn, which occurred in May 1948. Jesus then mentioned the generation which sees these things. A generation, as spoken of in Psalm 90:10, is a maximum of eighty years.

Add eighty to May 1948 and it gives us approximately May of 2028. Jesus stated that "this" generation would not expire before all the things He mentioned happened. Jesus mentions the beginning and the first part of the Great Tribulation as part of those things. However neither Matthew 24 nor Revelation 6 mentions more than the first day or days of the last half of the Great Tribulation. Therefore only the first portion of the Great Tribulation should be considered in the calculation.

Subtract the first half of the Great Tribulation, which is thought to be approximately three and a half years, from May 2028, which is approximately December 2024. This would seem to be very close to the latest possible start of the Great Tribulation. Jesus mentioned summer, a season, perhaps a general time period but not the day or hour. Considering these statements and seeing how information is sometimes hidden in plain sight, there could easily be more information which gives more specific insight. Jesus's statements seem clear yet give some leeway. Adding three years to 2024 would seem to be enough to include the unknown. All of this is based on Palm 90:10's mention of 70 or 80 years being a generation. If this is incorrect, the suggested timing will be wrong.

The day that the sacrifices are stopped you may choose to add 1,335 days to that date, which should be very close to the date of the rapture. Then find out the date Rosh Hashanah – the Feast of Trumpets Yom falls on that fall. Teruah – the Feast of Trumpets should be very close to that date. You then as always, have a goal to follow the Lord completely to that day. "How blessed is he who keeps waiting and attains to the 1,335 days!" (Dan. 12:12, NASB)

I don't think of the suggested timing of the events to be absolute but about 95% probable. It would not come as any surprise if more biblical insight is found and the dates of 2024 to 2027 are found to be wrong, though it does *seem* to be close to what Jesus taught. If you see lawlessness increase to the point that people are become unloving, if you see the Temple in Jerusalem rebuilt and the sacrifices start, you will then know how very close the Great Tribulation is—approximately three and a half years away.

How will you wager?

Yom Teruah – Rosh Hashanah – the Feast of Trumpets

Year	Month	Day
2022	Sept.	7th & 8th
2023	Sept.	26th & 27th
2024	Sept.	16th & 17th
2025	Oct.	3rd & 4th
2026	Sept.	23th & 24th
2027	Sept.	12th & 13th
2028	Oct.	2th & 3th
2029	Sept.	21st & 22nd
2030	Sept.	18th &19th
2031	Sept.	28th & 29th
2032	Sept.	18th & 19th
2033	Sept.	6th & 7th

2034	Sept.	24th & 25th
2035	Sept.	14th & 15th
2036	Oct.	4th & 5th
2037	Sept.	22nd & 23rd

These future dates of Yom Teruah – Rosh Hashanah – The Feast of Trumpets gleaned from Wikipedia. https://en.wikipedia.org/wiki/Jewish_and_Israel_holidays 2000-2050.

Briefly - if, if the timing previously discussed is correct then we should see the following events occurring in the not too distant future. If you learn that the Temple is being built, that there is a seven year (peace?) treaty and then the sacrifices are started, it will then be highly improbable that the Great Tribulation is - IMPENDING. The timing which follows is a best guess.

The building of the Temple starts by approximately 2020?

The seven year peace treaty signed near 2022?

The sacrifices start by 2022?

The sacrifices stopped in 2025?

The rapture most likely occurs before 2029?

24   How Bad Will It Be?

The worst suffering in history must be horrendous.

"And he will speak out against the Most High and wear down the saints of the Highest One, ..." (Dan. 7:25, NASB). He will likely make laws that will make it difficult to live, and hunt down Christians.

Whether through the common flu or Ebola or otherwise, millions, including Christians, may suffer death by pestilence. In addition the means are available for terrorists to purchase nuclear materials, bring them across our border, and construct a dirty bomb.

An EMP (electromagnetic pulse) weapon could destroy all the electronics in a large city. If China were to detonate a nuclear weapon a hundred miles in space above the United States, it would destroy almost all electronics in our country. The electricity to almost all homes would be out. The electronics that run your cell phone and your home landline phone would likely be out. The electronics that allow your car to run would be fried. The TV, VCR, BlackBerry, iPhone, and computer would be fried. Your lights would be out, your phone wouldn't work, your car wouldn't start, the microwave oven wouldn't work, and the refrigerator wouldn't work. The police cars' electronics are out and they won't start. The same is true for the ambulances and fire trucks. The grocery stores are closed, their registers won't work, the automatic sliding doors won't open, and the food in the freezers is thawing. No trucks are running, so the grocery stores are not receiving food. The tanker trucks won't run, therefore the gas stations don't receive any gasoline. That doesn't matter anyway since the electric fuel pumps that pump gas won't work. Their electronics are fried also. Many backup generators have also been burned up by the electromagnetic burst. If the generators were protected by a Faraday cage, their gasoline supply would soon run out. The effects would ripple across life as we know it—transport, retail, health care, and all of our jobs essentially would come to a halt. Some military equipment might be spared if it is sufficiently hard wired.

If there were a significant earthquake in the Midwest, on the New Madrid fault line, almost all bridges across the Mississippi River would be destroyed. Millions of homes and business could be destroyed. Tractor trailers with food and goods could not cross the river, at least until a branch of the military installed temporary bridges.

If there were a significant earthquake on the San Andreas fault or even worse, on Cascadia's Fault, it would be horrific. A great percentage of our economy would likely end, not considering even worse the loss of life. Jerry Thompson's book *Cascadia's Fault* describes its potential.

July 3, 2008, Fargo, ND, Barack Obama: "The problem is, is that the way Bush has done it over the past eight years is to take out a credit card from the bank of China in the name of our children, driving up our national debt from $5 trillion dollars for the first 42 presidents—number 43 added $4 trillion dollars by his lonesome, so that we now have over $9 trillion dollars of debt that we are going to have to pay back—$30,000 for every man woman and child. That's irresponsible, its unpatriotic" (http://leftofthemark.com/quote/barack-obama-bushs-deficit-spending-is-unpatriotic; 3/28/2016 www.cato.org/zimbabwe; 3/28/2016 fortune.com/2015/06/12zimbabwe-hyperinflation/; 3/28/2016 https://en.wikipedia.org/wiki/Hyperinflation_in_Zimbabwe: 4/7/2016 or try "Wikipedia" "hyperinflation" "Zimbabwe" 3/28/2016 www.globalfinancialdata.com 3/28/2016

After less than the eight years in office for Obama, the national debt has surpassed $19 trillion dollars, 10 trillion more dollars in debt in less than eight years. We are now in debt of over $58,000 per person. If we add college loans, mortgages, car loans, credit card debt, and other personal loans, our debt is much, much higher. The exact tipping point which might push the United States over the edge is not known. You can check the website www.usadebtclock.org 3/28/2016 for yourself.

The lava dome of the Yellowstone super volcano is rising. If Yellowstone erupted, it would also be a major disaster. It could shower down glasslike fibers over most of the United States. These fibers of glass would cut into our lungs. They would clog up the air filters in cars, shut down air travel, and so on. This is all a train wreck in slow motion. It is anyone's guess how long it will be until Yellowstone erupts. It is anyone's guess what will happen.

Yes, it is true, the first half of the Great Tribulation is not as bad as the last half. However, the entire period will be the greatest suffering in human history.

God's predicted event will likely be much, worse than most of us imagine. It will be interesting to see to what degree our personal perception of reality allows us to imagine the not-distant future. It doesn't even require a reading of the book of Revelation to hold an apocalyptic view. A group of professionals in the fields of economics, energy, plate tectonics (earthquakes, volcanos, tsunamis), agriculture, water, and AI (artificial intelligence), produced a for-TV program, *The Prophets of Doom*. These professionals and others have visions that are in some ways similar to the one in the book of Revelation.

Only continued advances in food production, fracking, horizontal drilling, and so on seem to have staved off the consequences of current trends—or is it Biblical timing? View *The Prophets of Doom* online for an idea of what might come our way. Though it is not from a biblical perspective, some of the events it describes may be similar (www.vidinfo.org/video/49198513/prophets-of-doom-2011-full-documentary-hist) 3/28/2016 or try the "history channel the prophets of doom" 3/28/2016 or "youtube the prophets of doom" 3/29/2016

"The sky is falling, the sky is falling." That response comes from some, and yet another perspective may lead to the same conclusion, in the historical view. One of the primary lessons of history is that change is constant and history repeats itself. Nations rise and nations fall. The sky *was* falling for them.

Historically, the larger a nation, population-wise and geographically, and the more diverse it is in terms of political views, races, religions, languages, organizations, and so on, the sooner that nation will fall. How does the United States stand in regard to these historical lessons?

Areas of a nation, that are geographically isolated may have fewer discussions with other parts of a country on important issues. TV and the Internet can help break divides or cause more separation; however, media may not replace the insight personal contact gives. When one group does not think about or respect others but simply assumes they themselves are correct, it can of course lead to conflict.

The larger the population, the more competition there will be for resources. With various languages, it becomes difficult to communicate. Differences that might have been resolved by simply listening to a news broadcast and understanding another view may not happen. What is a nasty criticism in one culture, such as an "OK" hand signal, is perfectly polite in another, but you can't even talk about it because neither party may know the other's language. How many people can learn all the languages and dialects now in the United States? Diversity can also have consequences. Embracing diversity can in some cases be a good thing, but not in every case. You don't think so? Invite a group of cannibals into your home for a vacation; embrace diversity.

Russia is spoken of in the Bible as the "bear," which is a Russian national symbol. There is almost no mention of the "eagle," representing the United States in the Bible. Why is the most powerful nation of the last days' time period given little to no biblical mention? Jeremiah 48:40, Ezekiel 17:7-11 and Daniel 7:4 might, again might, refer to America as the eagle. Will America fall by earthquake, EMP attack, a sociopolitical fall, economic collapse, or nuclear attack?

This may seem unrealistic. Yet nations rise and fall, and no matter what someone's political, spiritual, or economic view is, almost everyone seems to think the world is going crazy. As with the Rome Empire and other countries, the fall of America might not be as far off as we think.

25 Our Response

If we are living in the last days, is there anything we should do? Yes. "and let us consider how to stimulate one another to love and good deeds, 25 **not forsaking our own assembling together, as is the habit of some**, but encouraging one another; and all the more, as you see the day drawing near." (Heb. 10:24-25, NASB, EM). We should make a point of attending a local church that accurately teaches God's Word, if one is available.

If you can't get out of the house, it may be best to make one or more church organizations you see on TV your church. Then tithe to them. Charles Stanley, John Haggy, Perry Stone, *The 700 Club* with Pat Robertson, Rabbi Jonathan Cahn, Dr. James Merritt, Brian Houston, Dr. Michael Youssef, Ravi Zacharias and Greg Laurie are a few of those worthy of consideration.

Sharing our faith and telling others about Christ is necessary. "Everyone therefore who shall confess Me before men, I will also confess him before My Father who is in heaven. 33 "But whoever shall deny Me before men, I will also deny him before My Father who is in heaven." (Matt. 10:32–33, NASB). "He who is not with Me, is against Me; and he who does not gather with Me scatters." (Matt. 12:30, NASB). We need to be praising God, reading the Bible, praying to God, and doing these things daily. "Gather"—tell others about Christ and more.

In Matthew 10:10–14, Jesus sends his disciples out into the world to preach the gospel. You may want to consider this passage, asking if this teaching of Jesus is one you should to apply to your life.

"If I shut up the heavens so that there is no rain, or if I command the locust to devour the land, or if I send pestilence among My people, 14 and My people who are called by My name humble themselves and pray, and seek My face and turn from their wicked ways, then I will hear from heaven, will forgive their sin, and will heal their land." (2 Chron. 7:13–14, NASB).

It sounds like God holds Christians largely responsible for the moral and spiritual health of their country. Our prayer, humility, evangelism, and input on moral issues can have a positive effect on our nation's morality. If we who call ourselves Christians do not repent from our sins it is unlikely that our nation will stand.

"The only thing necessary for the triumph of evil is for good people to do nothing." —Edmund Burke

We should be writing and calling our congressmen. We should be teaching the Gospel.

Amos 1:3: "Thus says the Lord, "**For three transgressions of Damascus and for four I will not revoke its punishment, …**'" (NASB, EM)

Amos 1:6: "Thus says the Lord, "**For three transgression of Gaza and for four I will not revoke its punishment, …**" (NASB, EM)

Amos 1:9: "Thus says the Lord, "**For three transgressions of Tyre and for four I will not revoke its punishment, …**'" (NASB, EM)

Amos 1:11: "Thus says the Lord, "**For three transgressions of Edom and for four I will not revoke its punishment, …**" (NASB, EM)

Amos 1:13: "Thus says the Lord, "**For three transgressions of the sons of Ammon and for four I will not revoke its punishment, because they ripped open the pregnant women …**" (NASB, EM). Does this bring abortion to mind?

Amos 2:1: "Thus says the Lord, "**For three transgressions of Moab and for four I will not revoke its punishment, …**" (NASB, EM)

Amos 2:4: "Thus says the Lord, "**For three transgressions of Judah and for four I will not revoke its punishment, <u>because they rejected the</u>**

law of the Lord, and have not kept His statutes; their lies also have led them astray, ..." (NASB, EM)

Amos 2:6: "Thus says the Lord, "**For three transgressions of Israel and for four I will not revoke its punishment, because they sell the righteous for money and the needy for a pair of sandals. ...**'" (NASB, EM). There may be companies that this passage may remind us of, who loan money at interest rates that can enslave the poor for years or for a lifetime.

How many sins is America guilty of - Idolatry, Pride, Fornication, Adultery, Greed, Hedonism, Pornography, Theft, Slothfulness, Abortion, Not Forgiving, Arrogance, Selfishness, Unloving, Manipulation, Enslavement, Pimping, Gossip, Slander, Not Respecting the Sabbath, Not Reading the Bible, Not Tithing 10% of gross, Not Evangelizing for Christ, Not Praising God, Neglecting God and more? Will we repent?

At one time most of America's laws seemed to be in accordance with Biblical law. As America's laws changed, making more and more of those things God mentions as transgressions legal, it drives our nation farther from God. More people seem to be engaging in activity opposed by God. How far off are we from being like Sodom and Gomorrah?

Where is the United States in God's eyes? Rabbi Jonathan Cahn produced the DVD *Isaiah 9:10*, in which he talks about the harbinger, which Israel experienced long ago. Rabbi Cahn compares the harbinger, a warning from God, to the events of 9/11. Rabbi Cahn's comparison on several points is convincing. It seems God has sent a warning, or more than one warning, that He is removing His protection due to America's rebellion against Him.

"...Now **appoint a king for us to judge us** like all the nations.".... 7 And the Lord said to Samuel, "Listen to the voice of the people in regard to all that they say to you, for they have not rejected you, but they have rejected Me from being king over them. ... 9 "Now then, listen to their voice;

however, **you shall solemnly warn them and tell them of the procedure of the king who will reign over them.**" (1 Sam. 8:5, 7, 9, NASB, EM).

"...I have appointed a king over you." (1 Sam. 12:1, NASB).

It is as though God said, "You want a king? I will give you a king, but you won't like it." Is there any chance that this has happened in a similar way in America in recent years?

President Barack Obama has said, "If in fact, I could solve all these problems without passing laws in Congress, then I would do so. But we're a nation of laws, that's part of our tradition. And so the easy way out is to try to yell and pretend like I can do something without violating our laws" (www.al.com/news/ index.ssf/2014/11/22_quotes_from_obama_saying_he.html). 3/29/2016

Obama was also was heard to comment, "That's the good thing about being president; I can do whatever I want" (hotair.com/headlines/archives/2014/02/11thats-the-good-thing-about-being-president-i-can-do-whatever-i-want; click "Read the Article") 3/29/2016.

The office of president does not, of course, give authority to a president to do whatever he wants. 'When it comes to "President Barack Obama's plan to take the immigration system in his own hands is a daring test of the limits of presidential power'" (www.cnn.com/2014/11/20politics/immigration-obama-legal). 3/29/2016

In June 2007, speaking to CBS, Obama said, "Whatever we once were, we are no longer a Christian nation—at least, not just. We are also a Jewish nation, a Muslim nation, a Buddhist nation, and a Hindu nation, and a nation of non-believers" (www.thenewamerican.com/usnews/politics/item/2576-obama). 3/29/2016 Obama's view is that "we do not consider ourselves a Christian nation or a Jewish nation or a Muslim nation" (www.americanthinker.com/articles/2009/04/obamas-christian-nation-1.html). 3/29/2016

"But a certain one of them, Caiaphas, who was high priest that year, said to them, "You know nothing at all, 50 nor do you take into account that it is expedient for you that one man should die for the people, and that the whole nation should not perish." 51 Now this **he did not say on his own initiative**; but being high priest that year, he prophesied that Jesus was going to die for the nation," (John 11:49–51, NASB, EM).

In Obama's statement that included the phrase "we are no longer a Christian nation,". The words "no longer" mean it was once true but isn't now—that is, previously the United States was a Christian nation, but now it is not. At one time many of the people in the United States seemed to think we were a Christian nation. The number of people who considered themselves Christians outnumbered those who claimed other religions.

It seems clear that Obama was saying, we are a nation of a number of a number of religions. Obama definitely meant what he said, stating that our national identity as Christian has changed. Now we are no longer a Christian nation but a nation of numerous religions.

Did God plant the phrase "the United States is no longer a Christian nation" in Obama's mouth, prophetically, as He did with Caiaphas, though not as high priest as Caiaphas was? No doubt there are Christians in the United States, but are we a Christian nation? Did God plant this as prophecy by using a statement that Barak Obama thought?

Why is this important?

"Now the Philistines took the ark of God and brought it from Ebenezer to Ashdod. 2 Then the Philistines took the ark of God and brought it to the house of Dagon, and set it by Dagon. 3 When the Ashdodites arose early the next morning, behold, Dagon had fallen on his face to the ground before the ark of the Lord. So they took Dagon and set him in his place again. 4 But when they arose early the next morning, behold, Dagon had fallen on his face to the ground before the ark of the Lord. And the head of Dagon and both the palms of his hands were cut off on the threshold; only the trunk of Dagon was left to him. … 6 Now the hand of the Lord was heavy on the Ashdodites, and He ravaged them and smote them with tumors, both Ashdod and its territories." (1 Sam.5:1-4, 6 partial, NASB).

"You shall have no other gods before Me." (Exod.20:3, NASB).

These passages state that God will not tolerate other "gods," period. We are not to have any interest in other religions, nor participation in their services, nor making an activity or entertainment more important than God. As he states in Isaiah 45:5, "I am the Lord, and there is no other; …." (NASB). In Isaiah 45 and 46, this idea is stated six times. " …other gods provoke Me to anger." (Jer. 32:29, NASB).

President Obama said at the national prayer breakfast, on February 6, 2009, "I didn't become a Christian until many years later, when I moved to the south side of Chicago after college …" (http://www.huffingtonpost.com/2012/02/21obama-religious-quotes_n_1292116.html). 3/29/2016

Obama: "The sweetest sound I know is the Muslim call to prayer." www.nowtheendbegins.com/40-mind-blowing-quotes-barack-hussein-obama-islalm-christianity/ 3/13/2016

Obama: "The future must not belong to those who slander the prophet of Islam" (http://freedomoutpost.com/2013/09/contrast-barack-obamas-quotes-islam-quotes,christianity/). 3/29/2016

Jesus: "No one can serve two masters; for either he will hate the one and love the other, or he will hold to one and despise the other. …" (Matt. 6:24, NASB).

President Obama celebrated the Muslim holiday of Ramadan on June 23, 2015. (www.huffingtonpost.com/2015/06/23/obama-white-house-ramadan_n_7644614.hmtl). 3/29/2016

Whom does President Obama serve?

Obama: "I believe that there are many paths to the same place, and that is a belief that there is a higher power, a belief that we are connected as a people" (http://freedomoutpost.com/2013/09/contrast-barack-obamas-quote-islam-quotes,christianity/). 3/29/2016

If it is true that the United States is now a nation of numerous religions, what does that mean for those of us living in America?

"I am the Lord, that is My name; I will not give My glory to another, ..." (Isa. 42:8, NASB).

"... And My glory I will not give to another." (Isa. 48:11, NASB).

God does not share his glory. "Jesus said to him, "I am the way, and the truth, and the life; <u>no one comes to the Father, but through Me.</u>'" (John 14:6, NASB, EM). President Obama's comments are the complete opposite of what scripture says, as he stated "there are many paths to the same place."

It is interesting that President Obama mentions his Christianity while denying basic tenets of Christianity. Where is President Obama's allegiance? Like Christianity, Islam is exclusive and will not accept any other religion. The beheadings by ISIS of those who hold any other religious view is evidence of Islam's exclusive view. Does the president realize that some of these religions he seems to embrace are completely exclusive, in complete opposition? How can President Obama hold conflicting views? The President should see the conflict. To be clear, I am not stating that Obama is or is not a Muslim or a Christian or something else. Does President Obama understand? Is Obama delusional, is he lying, both or what otherwise?

The concept of a harbinger in the *Isaiah 9:10* DVD have been mentioned because they seem to deliver a similar message to what part of Barack Obama's statement did. Just as God used Caiaphas, the high priest, God may have used Barack Obama to deliver a message to us—a warning, in the same way that a harbinger is a warning. Will we repent or suffer the consequences?

It is approximately 93 million miles from the earth to the sun, quite a road trip. Despite the great distance, light makes the trip in approximately eight minutes, traveling at approximately 186,000 miles per second. Not miles per hour, but miles per second.

There are about 7 billion people living on earth. The Milky Way Galaxy, which we live in, contains about 100 billion stars. Even though light travels at about 186,000 miles per second, it takes light about 100,000 years to travel from one side of our galaxy to the other.

Light traveling from the farthest parts of the universe that scientific instruments can detect undergoes "red shift." By some means, light is stretched by its long trip and becomes a bit more red. The best estimates are that the most distant light has traveled for 14 billion years before arriving at Earth. God says, "For My thoughts are not your thoughts, neither are your ways My ways," declares the Lord. 9 "For as the heavens are higher than the earth, so are My ways higher than your ways, and My thoughts than your thoughts." (Isa. 55:8-9, NASB).

The thought is humbling, which is just what we need. We must humble ourselves before God and obey, which is very little to ask considering what God has promised.

26   No Action Taken in Faith or Actions Done in Faith

Is there anything that Christians should do to provide for their families and/or other Christians in the time to come? Should you work hard to pay off your home, build a small orphanage, purchase a better vehicle, buy gold, build a small nursing home or a retirement home? Don't just jump in, think about it thoroughly. Why do any of these? Could you do so without going in debt? Under what circumstances might any of these be the right thing for you, if any? None of these might be right for you.

There are many Christians who believe that there is nothing for Christians to do, as we are to live by faith. "BUT MY RIGHTOUS ONE SHALL LIVE BY FAITH; AND IF HE SHRINKS BACK, MY SOUL HAS NO PLEASURE IN HIM." (Heb. 10:38, NASB). The entire chapter of Hebrews 11 continues speaking of things done by faith. Basing our lives on faith is taught throughout the Bible.

Numerous times in the Bible, God tells us to wait. Do we wait—for example for God to bring manna for us to eat? Do we seek a word from the Lord to tell us exactly what we should do? Or do we see our circumstances, consider what God's Word says, and take action based on God's Word, which is acting in faith also?

Some might cite James 2:18: "But someone may well say, "You have faith, and I have works; show me your faith without the works, and I will show you my faith by my works." (NASB). Whatever we do, we should first turn to inquire of God. If our works do not break God's law, if we give the credit to God, if we do have faith, if what is done is purposed for good, and if we thank God, then it is at least less likely that God will find fault with us.

Yet how long do we wait for an answer? Are there instances in which God is thinking, "I have already told you in My Word?"

"But if anyone does not provide for his own, and especially for those of his household, he has denied the faith, and is worse than an unbeliever." (1 Tim.5:8, NASB). What provision is spoken of, and is there a limit to what it covers?

"Go to the ant, O sluggard, observe her ways and **be wise**," (Prov. 6:6, NASB, EM).

"Listen, my son, and **be wise**, and direct your heart in the way." (Prov. 23:19, NASB, EM).

"Behold, I send you forth as sheep in the midst of wolves: **be ye therefore wise** as serpents, and harmless as doves." (Matt. 10:16, KJV, EM).

Yet we can't just say, "I will be wise," since wisdom is a gift. We can use the degree of wisdom we do have, and stop doing things that we know are foolish.

"So give Thy servant an understanding heart to judge Thy people to discern between good and evil. For who is able to judge this great people of Thine?" 10 And it was pleasing in the sight of the Lord that Solomon had asked this thing. 11 And God said to him, "Because you have asked this thing and have not asked for yourself long life, nor have asked riches for yourself, nor have you asked for the life of your enemies, but have asked for yourself discernment to understand justice, 12 behold, I have done according to your words. Behold, I have given you a wise and discerning heart, so that there has been no one like you before you, nor shall one like you arise after you.'" (1 Kings 3:9–12, NASB).

God must also have given Solomon enough wisdom to ask wisely. Pray for wisdom.

"But if any of you lacks wisdom, let him ask of God, who gives to all men generously and without reproach, and it will be given to him." (James 1:5, NASB).

There are those who will do something out of fear, which is the opposite of faith. There are also those who believe God and are doing what they think God's word would have them do which is faith.

Just as those who believe there is nothing to do, should not be criticized, so also those who believe they should be actively doing things should not be criticized unless there is a true word from God. Both can be said to be acting out of faith, if it is not done out of fear. Has God been guiding one or the other or both? For as God's ways are higher than the earth, do we know what God wants from someone else specifically?

"If anyone supposes that he knows anything, he has not yet known as he ought to know." (1 Cor. 8:2, NASB).

In Luke 17:26–30, Jesus said it will be just as it was during the days of Noah and Lot. Is there anything that may be inferred from Noah and Lot's time, as to whether we should do anything out of the ordinary or not?

"Then the men said to Lot, "Whom else have you here? A son-in-law, and your sons, and your daughters, and whoever you have in the city, **bring** *them* **out of the place**; 13 for we are **about to destroy this place**, because their outcry has become so great before the Lord that the Lord has sent us **to destroy it**." 14 And Lot went out and spoke to his sons-in-law, who were to marry his daughters, and said, "Up, get out of this place, for **the Lord will destroy the city**," But he appeared to his sons-in-law to be jesting. 15 And when morning dawned, the **angels urged Lot**, saying, "**Up, take your wife and your two daughters,** who are here, **lest you be swept away in the punishment of the city**." 16 <u>**But he hesitated**</u>. So the **men seized his hand and the hand of his wife and the hands of his daughters,** for the compassion of the Lord was upon him; and they brought him out, and put him outside the city. 17 And it came about when they had brought them outside, that one said, "**Escape for your life!** Do not look behind you, and do not stay anywhere in the valley; **escape to the mountains, lest you be swept away**." 18 But Lot said to them, "**Oh no,** my lords! …" 22 "**Hurry, escape** there, for I cannot do anything until you arrive there." Therefore the name of the town was called Zoar. 23 The sun had risen over the earth when Lot came to Zoar. 24 Then the Lord rained on Sodom and Gomorrah brimstone and fire from the Lord out of heaven," (Gen. 19:12-18, 22-24, NASB, EM).

Lot is told three times that Sodom is about to be destroyed. Lot is told to get his family out of Sodom. Lot is urged to get out of town. Lot is warned that if he stays he may be "swept away"—that is, killed, just as someone sweeps dust away.

What does Lot do? Lot hesitates. Lot is a righteous man (Gen. 18:26). Lot is spared. Lot believes God, and yet he waits; he hesitates to the point that the angels (also called men) grab the hands of Lot and his family and all but drag them out of town to save their lives. Lot arrives at Zoar and fire and brimstone—probably meteorites—hail down on Sodom.

Lot and his family (except for his wife) were very fortunate to get out of Sodom alive, since Lot did not do what he was told immediately. God was gracious. God gave Lot something to do, something simple—get out of town. In Lot's case, this was all that was required for Lot and his family to be saved.

"Then God said to Noah, "The end of all flesh has come before Me; for the earth is filled with violence because of them; and behold, I am about to destroy them with the earth. 14 **Make for yourself an ark of gopher wood; ...**" (Gen. 6:13, 14, partial, NASB, EM). The ark was approximately 450 feet long (longer than a football field), approximately 75 feet wide, and 45 feet high. That is what God told Noah "to do"—to save his family and two of every kind of animal.

Despite the great amount of work Noah did, Noah could not do it all. God brought the animals and closed the door after Noah and his family boarded. Even if someone thinks there is something for them to do, trust in God is essential. Lot had it easy. Noah had a huge boat to build, a large undertaking.

These examples are not intended to solely support a proactive position or the passive position. There doesn't seem to be anything wrong with attempting to convince people that your position is correct. However, caution is wise for those who might consider rebuking others.

"Now it happened at the end of two full years that Pharaoh had a dream, and behold, he was stranding by the Nile. 2 And lo, from the Nile there came up seven cows, sleek and fat; and they grazed in the marsh grass. 3 Then behold, seven other cows came up after them from the Nile, ugly and gaunt, and they stood by the other cows on the bank of the Nile. 4 And the ugly and gaunt cows ate up the seven sleek and fat cows. Then Pharaoh awoke." (Gen. 41:1–4, NASB).

"Now it came about in the morning that his spirit was troubled, so he sent and called for all the magicians of Egypt, and all its wise men. And Pharaoh told them his dreams, but there was no one who could interpret them to Pharaoh. ... 14 Then Pharaoh sent and called for Joseph, and they hurriedly brought him out of the dungeon; and when he had shaved himself and changed his clothes, he came to Pharaoh. 15 And Pharaoh said to Joseph, "I have had a dream, but no one can interpret it; and I have heard it said about you, that when you hear a dream you can interpret it." ... 25 Now Joseph said to Pharaoh, ... 29 "Behold, seven years of great abundance are coming in all the land of Egypt; 30 and after them seven years of famine will come, and all the abundance will be forgotten in the land of Egypt; and the famine will ravage the land.'" (Gen. 41:8, 14-15, 29-30, NASB).

"So Pharaoh said to Joseph, "Since God has informed you of all this, **there is no one so discerning and wise as you are.** 40 "You shall be over my house, and according to your command all my people shall do homage; only in the throne I will be greater than you." 41 And Pharaoh said to Joseph, "See I have set you over all the land of Egypt." (Gen. 41:39–41, EM).

This was an honor for Joseph; however, it was also now his responsibility, his job, to save all of Egypt. Joseph might have been severely disciplined if he had failed to provide food for Egypt.

"So he gathered all the food of *these* seven years which occurred in the land of Egypt, and placed the food in the cities; he placed in every city the food from its own surrounding fields." (Gen. 41:48, NASB).

Joseph was successful and Egypt was saved; as the passage says, it was due to the gifts God gave Joseph, like wisdom. The passage says God informed Joseph about the dream. There is no clear mention in the English that God told Joseph to do anything. It only mentions that Joseph was wise and acted.

If we are to go through times similar to those experienced by Joseph, how should we respond? Did Joseph respond out of fear, faith, and wisdom, or just faith and wisdom? There is nothing to suggest that Joseph was fearful.

Scripture has given us insight into similar things that will almost certainly soon occur, in Matthew 24, Revelation 6, and other passages. So do we walk by faith and do nothing, or do we do something out of our belief—faith and wisdom?

If your home is paid for, home insurance and life insurance are not mandatory by law, at least last I heard. Home insurance is for those unpredictable catastrophes that can catch anyone off guard. Disability insurance is normally not for an event we know will happen. When we buy home insurance, life insurance, and disability insurance, do we do so out of fear or wisdom? Does it mean we don't trust God?

Many who think they should take action, as Joseph did, are responding to what they are convinced will occur. If we purchase insurance that is not mandatory by law, should we criticize those who read God's Word and react in a way so as to provide for their families, as God has said a man should do? (1 Tim. 5:8).

Solomon said, "Divide your portion to seven, or even to eight, for you do not know what misfortune may occur on the earth." (Eccles. 11:2, NASB). Solomon may not have been the originator of the concept of diversification of assets, but he did understand the concept. If you have all your eggs in one basket or all your grain in one barn, and that basket or barn is struck by lightning and burns, likely all of your assets will be gone. In a similar way, taking action like Joseph did, storing the food grown in each city where harvested, is a diversification of assets or insurance.

You are watching TV when your program is interrupted by a weather bulletin. An F5 tornado has been spotted in your area. You are warned to go immediately to your basement, if you have one.

You open your front door and see the violent tornado ripping homes apart and headed your way. You do have a basement. Do you yell to your family and lead them to the basement quickly? Or do you call your family to the front door and point out the killer tornado and then say God will protect you? Did God tell you He would protect you from the tornado?

In Matthew 4:6, Satan suggests to Jesus that He jump off the point of the temple, saying the angels will save Him. "Jesus said to him, "On the other hand, it is written, 'You shall not put the Lord your God to the test.'" (Matt. 4:7, NASB). Are we in a similar situation? If we react to the weather report or personally seeing a tornado, how should we react to what Jesus has said?

A few of numerous passages that encourage us to wait for the Lord:

"Yet those who wait for the Lord will gain new strength; They will mount up *with* wings like eagles, they will run and not get tired, They will walk and not become weary." (Isa. 40:31, NASB).

"…Those who hopefully wait for Me will not be put to shame." (Isa. 49:23, NASB).

"The Lord is good to those who wait for Him, to the person who seeks Him. 26 It is good that he waits silently for the salvation of the Lord." (Lam. 3:25–26, NASB).

For those who are sure that they hear from God, they should almost certainly wait to hear from the Lord. Could there be times when God expects those who do not hear God audibly to simply obey His Word in the Bible?

There are many of us who think that if God is communicating in some way other than the Bible, we are not aware of it, or we seldom think we have heard from the Lord. It would probably be best for us to spend a week or two in prayer and fasting, asking to hear from Him. Fortunately, if our ears are too dull to hear, we still have the Bible to consult.

The point of all of this is that we should be very careful not to assume we know what God has in mind for others. There may be many ways to Jesus; however, Jesus is the only way to God. In the same way, God may plan different ways for each of us to handle what is to come. Other than spiritually, our lives are so different that it is nearly impossible to say you should do this or do that.

If you intend to be pro-active, <u>if you are well off</u>, own your own home or R.V., and have invested well in bonds, stock, IRA's, etc., you might want to consider diversifying another way. These specific things may be helpful whether the Great Tribulation occurs or no. You are likely saving for what you will need in retirement, such as heating, cooling, and lights. You might consider American made solar and or wind power. If you install solar and/or a wind turbine and for instance the market were to collapse, you would not lose that amount of money and would have your own power. An EMP burst could take out solar and wind power, unless it was hardened – protected by a Faraday cage and the wiring was in grounded copper or perhaps steel pipe. Being off grid would isolate your solar system from EMP effects that could come through power lines. This diversification is like buying your heating, cooling, and light power in advance. If there are no emergency situations, then you have not lost anything, assuming the solar system satisfies your need. Solar and wind turbines can of course also be mounted on construction trailers for example, if done wisely. Solar or wind power might work for you or it may not; only you can decide. It would not seem to be wise to go into debt to purchase solar. Solar seems to be for those who have the means.

To provide the best service for customers while I was driving for UPS, there was seldom a moment to stop and talk. A wave and a smile normally had to be enough. One Christmas there was a package for a home I had never delivered to. Only on a few occasions had I seen an elderly lady at this home. As I approached the front door, I noticed some small holes in the molding around the front door, and this was important. The lady, a widow, answered the door and I addressed her. "Good afternoon, I have a package for you, and by the way, from the looks of the molding around your door, it looks like you have termites."

This was the second home on which I had seen these small holes, and termites were confirmed in the prior home. The woman answered smiling, "Yes it does." The answer seemed odd, yet a reply to her response could be considered rude. A neighbor called a government agency after seeing the garage door continually open during the winter. Without a number of contacts it had not been possible to recognize Alzheimer's disease. A two hundred and fifty thousand dollar home had termites, a leaking roof, and a garage door that would not close since only one outlet in the home worked. The home had to be bulldozed. Her children lived out of town and seemingly had little contact. A neighbor learned she had been sleeping under the kitchen table to keep dry and in the winter used a small space heater for warmth.

A typical roof lasts for about 15 to 20 years. If you expect to live in your home for sixty years, you will probably replace the roofing as least twice. For those of you who can afford it, a quality stainless steel (enough nickel and chromium and heavy enough gauge) roof could last, not only through your life time but your children's and great grandchildren's life times as well.

A stainless steel will cost more than one typical roof installation. Yet one installation of stainless steel roofing might not cost as much as the original roof and three to five replacement roofs. If you can afford it, it might be a wise investment. Stainless steel roofing may be available in colors or anodized, yet at more cost. The walls of the woman's home would likely have held up the roof for the rest of her life span, if the roof had been stainless steel, keeping her warm and dry.

It is a matter of whether the money is available and is stainless steel roofing is a priority. All of the advantages of a stainless steel roof may not be obvious. One example; should the roof become damaged esthetically, it is of value when recycled. If you pay for a stainless steel roof you can't lose that money in the market. You have in a sense paid for reroofing in advance, while protecting some assets. Again it would probably unwise to go in debt to make such purchase. A stainless steel roof is something else that can be of value even if there were not an apocalypse.

27   A Family Decision

"The word of the Lord also came to me saying, 2 "You shall not take a wife for yourself nor have sons or daughters in this place." 3 For thus says the Lord concerning the sons and daughters born in this place, and concerning their mothers who bear them, and their fathers who beget them in this land: 4 "They will die of deadly diseases, they will not be lamented or buried; they will be as dung on the surface of the ground and come to an end by sword and famine, and their carcasses will become food for the birds of the sky and for the beasts of the earth." (Jer. 16:1-4, NASB).

Jeremiah was a prophet, so he must have had great importance to God, as all of God's people are, and yet he was told not to marry, nor have children. Will the conditions we are to face be any better than those of Jeremiah?

This is an extremely personal decision, which is not to be made lightly. Only you are in a position to make such a decision, and you should, pray and think wisely as to how confident you are as to what the near future holds.

"Now at that time Michael, the great prince who stands guard over the sons of your people, will arise. And there will be a time of distress such as never occurred since there was a nation until that time; …" (Dan. 12:1, NASB).

"for then there will be a great tribulation, such as has not occurred since the beginning of the world until now, nor ever shall. 22 "And unless those days had been cut short, no life would have been saved; …" (Matt. 24:21–22, NASB).

Although Jeremiah may have been spared some suffering, there is nothing to indicate that Jeremiah did not have great suffering. Jesus says the times that those of us who are still alive will see, will be the worst suffering in history. We must walk by faith. Does faith trump wisdom, or do faith and wisdom walk hand in hand? In the times we face, would it be wise to apply God's statement to Jeremiah today? The decisions are between you and God.

"But woe to those who are with child and to those nurse babes in those days!" (Matt. 24:19, NASB). Is this just for those in Judea in Israel?

"If we say that we have no sin, we are deceiving ourselves, and the truth is not in us." (1 John 1:8, NASB).

"All the sinners of My people will die by the sword, those who say, 'The calamity will not overtake or confront us.'" (Amos 9:10, NASB).

28   Filthy Lucre & Contrasting Views

Some suggest that we should purchase gold or silver out of wisdom and faith, due to what God's Word says will occur. Others say the purchase of gold or silver is done out of fear. There is little difference between what Joseph did after Pharaoh put him in charge in Egypt and the decision to own or not to own intrinsic currency. This is simply making provision for the future in a different way. Gold and silver are forms of trade, as is paper currency. However, paper has no intrinsic value; it is just paper.

"For the love of money is a root of all sorts of evil, and some by longing for it have wandered away from the faith, and pierced themselves with many a pang." (1 Tim. 6:10, NASB). The passage says the "love" of money is what is bad, evil. Money itself is similar to a collection of tools; it is increments of something we use in trade, as a tool, for various things we need. It is how we use money and not to love money that is important, of course.

Solomon the wisest man to live:

"Take my instruction, and not silver, and knowledge rather than choicest gold." (Prov. 8:10, NASB).

"How much better it is to get wisdom than gold! And to get understanding is to be chosen above silver." (Prov. 16:16, NASB).

And yet Solomon, the wisest man to ever live, had gold. King Solomon says in Ecclesiastes 2:8 "Also, I collected for myself silver and gold, ..." (NASB).

Solomon seems to have understood that it is the "love" of money that is evil. It is how we use money that is important—to tithe, give to the poor, support our families, and glorify God.

Gold is no worse than paper money or money in the bank. The only difference between gold and silver, in comparison to paper money, is that during hyperinflation, paper money becomes worthless. Money in the bank—which is only positive and negative charges in computers—also becomes worthless. Gold, silver, even nickels, dimes, and quarters in your change jar should hold some value, for a while.

When your money loses a lot of value quickly, it is hyperinflation. Think it can't happen? It already has, in the past.

The excessive printing of money could lead to hyperinflation, in which case a hammer which might now cost $20.00 at 8:00am could cost $50.00 at lunch and $100.00 by 5:00pm. Hyperinflation has previously occurred in Zimbabwe, Germany, and Hungary. Deflation, the increase in value of our currency, is considered to be more likely than inflation by some analyzing our economic position in the United States. On the other hand our debt is rising rapidly. A hammer might be good as gold. (injesus. com/message-archives/Christian-living/alament/hyperinflation-by-britt-im-asking-you-by; 3/29/2016 https://www.globalfinancialdata.com/gfdblog/?p=2382). 3/29/2016

Does faith throw wisdom out the window, or do faith and wisdom go hand in hand? Solomon had the greatest wisdom, gold, and faith. Having faith and wisdom is clearly best.

Again, we should be cautious about rebuking someone who has money but does not love money and does not have the same view of money as ourselves. God may have a different plan for them.

There are things that Solomon did that we should avoid, such as having concubines. Solomon clearly was not perfect, Solomon, like all of us, sinned. Life was very difficult in Solomon's day, and his possession of concubines may have saved their lives. This does not justify Solomon acquiring concubines. In Ecclesiastes 2:8 Solomon mentions that he "collected" concubines. There is no mention that God said Solomon's possession of concubines was permissible. Solomon may have suffered a family crisis for his actions as King David did after his actions of taking Bathsheba. See Eccl. 1:13, 17 & 2:1,3 Did Solomon desire to sin or test himself?

Could it be that God gave Solomon the greatest wisdom in history, and did not stop Solomon's acquisition of gold, concubines etc., so that Solomon could say with great wisdom, " ...Vanity of vanities! All is vanity." (Eccles. 1:2, NASB). To paraphrase what Solomon may have meant: 'I tried it all, and I can tell you, to live as I did will not give you satisfaction. You may think these things will make you happy; however, they will not fulfill you. I know. I tried it all. Only God satisfies." "The conclusion, when all has been heard, *is*: fear God and keep His commandments, because this *applies* to every person." (Eccl.12:13, NASB).

God, speaking of Abraham and his descendants, said, "And I will bless those who bless you, and the one who curses you I will curse. ..." (Gen. 12:3, NASB). We have a unique opportunity in history to bless God's original people during one of the most critical times in history. We can give as we have means to feed and clothe the needy in Israel, and bring back to Israel those who are old and being persecuted in other countries. You can give to:

International Fellowship of Christians and Jews
PO Box 96105
Washington, DC 20090–6105
ifcj.org

Another unique opportunity, which hasn't occurred for about two thousand years, is available to us. The Temple has not stood in Israel for approximately two thousand years. In Haggai 1:3, God says it is time for His house—the Temple—to be rebuilt, in a sense a representation of God's glory. In Haggai 2:3 speaks of the Temple of God as not being as glorious as it had been. Haggai 2:7 tells how God will have the nations involved in making the Temple glorious.

On this Web site, you can see the objects of service that will be in the Temple, you must log in. Will we help make it glorious? We can give to:

The Temple Mt. Institute
PO Box 31876
Jerusalem, Israel 91317
www.templeinstitute.org/templemount.htm

Thoughts of all the suffering to come during the first portion of the Great Tribulation can be overwhelming and depressing. We however have a great hope in Christ. We already know the outcome, which is eternal life in paradise and that Christ is always with those who have committed to Him. Continually keeping that is mind should help us through whatever suffering is to come. May God bless you in every way, to help you, your family and others during these times and help you to glorify God thru Christ Jesus. Come, Lord, Come.

Notes

Chapter 3. You Can't Know When the Great Tribulation—Apocalypse— or the Rapture Will Occur?

1. *The Creator and the Cosmos*, by Hugh Ross, Nav Press. Colorado Springs, Colorado 80935. Copyright 1993, 1995, 2001, by Reasons to Believe.

1. *The Science of God*, by Gerald L. Schroeder, Originally published: New York : Free Press, copyright 1997; *Rare Earth*, by Peter D. Ward and Donald Brownlee, Copernicus Books, Copyright 2000 Springer Science + Business Media, LLC, New York, NY.

2. *Genetic Entropy & The Mystery of the Genome*, by Dr. J.C. Sanford, Copyright 2005 Dr. John C. Sanford, Published by Elim Publishing, Lima, New York.

3. *Signature in the Cell*, by Stephen C. Meyer, Harper One, Harper Collins, New York, NY, Copyright 2009 by Stephen C. Meyer.

Chapter 5. Coming of Age

1. The concept of establishing a time period using Daniel 12:4 comes from Hal Lindsay, *The Late Great Planet Earth (p. 89)*, Zondervan, Grand rapids, Michigan, Copyright 1970 by Zondervan.

2. Lindsey, *Late Great Planet Earth*, p. 53.

3. Lindsey, *Late Great Planet Earth*, p. 54.

Chapter 9. Putting the Puzzle Together

1. Peter Ward and Donald Brownlee, *Rare Earth* (New York: Springer Science & Business Media, 2000), pp. 18–19.

Chapter 12. The Blood Moons

1. Thanks to Mark Blitz, El SHADDAI Ministries (www. elshaddaiministries.us) resources are available.

2. https:/en:Wikipedia.org/wiki/Lists_of_lunar_eclipses 3/3/2016 https:/en,Wikipedia.org/wiki/Lunar_eclipse 3/3/2016 https:// en.wikipedia.org/Lists_of_solar_eclipses 3/3/2016

3. Pastor John Hagee, jhm.org, www.faithcenteredresources.com/

Chapter 23. What Is Soon to Come: Why 2027?

1. Jonathan Chan, *The Mystery of the Seventh Shemitah: The Mystery of the Shemitah VI* (Lodi, NJ: Hope of the World, 2013), DVD.

References

Very few of us can personally know the authors of the following resources. However, we have an opportunity to see a few of them on TV and can tell they are really great people. My confidence is high that the same can be said for the rest.

Resources on the Web

Britt Gillette at brittgillette.com, *End Times Bible Prophecy*. Read "A Christian Examination of Bible Prophecy and Emerging Technology." Britt has articles on prophecies. Britt also has articles on atomic printing and other emerging technology, if these are still online.

Mark Blitz, *El Shaddi Ministries*, www.elshaddiministries.us. Mark may have been the first to bring the four blood moon sequences to light.

119 Ministries, at 119ministries.com. Information on the blood moons and other biblical topics.

Books on the Cosmological Fine Tuning

Hugh Ross, PhD, The Creator and the Cosmos, Copyright 1993,1995,2001 by Reasons To Believe, 731 E. Arrow Hwy. Glendora, CA. 91740 One of the most detailed books on the Cosmological Fine Tuning, offering a large number of fine-tuning factors; in addition, the importance of many of the factors is discussed. A favorite book.

Gerald L. Schroeder, BS, MS, PhD, MIT, The Science of God. Copyright 1997 New York: Free Press 1997. Schroeder looks at the probability of life arising by chance, and a look at the fossil record. Schroeder has one of the most interesting looks at time in regard to the days in Genesis, based on the Jewish text. One of the most important points is the length of time that passed from the time the earth cooled until life appears in the fossil record. A great book. Also see *The Hidden Face of God*.

Peter D. Ward and Donald Brownlee, Rare Earth. Copyright 2000 Springer Science and Business Media LLC, 233 Spring Street, New York,: 10013 USA. Ward and Brownlee explain the CO2 recycling system mentioned in the chapter "Not By Chance" A relatively easy read regarding some Cosmological Fine Tuning factors, taking time to explain the fine tuning involving these factors.

Biological Fine Tuning Factors

Dr. J. C. Sanford, Genetic Entropy & The Mystery of the Genome. Copyright 2005, Published by Elim Publishing, Lima, Ny. Another interesting read. Sanford explains that our DNA is poly-functional, therefore poly-constrained, and therefore in a state of entropy. This has implications regarding evolution that are very interesting.

Stephen C. Meyer, PhD, Signature in the Cell: DNA and the Evidence for Intelligent Design. Copyright 2009. Published by New York: Harper Collins, 10 East 53rd Street, Ny. The specific information which was referred to is in chapter 9, "End and Odds", on pages 210-213. A deep look, for some of us, into some complex problems that face life evolving by chance, including relationships between proteins, RNA, and DNA. One of the most interesting points regards the symposium at the Wistar Institute. This involves the probability of chains of 150 amino acids randomly forming into the functional proteins necessary to form a simple one-celled organism, and then those proteins forming that microorganism by chance. It is staggering.

Other Valuable Resources

Pastor John Hagee, *The Coming Four Blood Moons*, DVD, available from www.jhm.org. Pastor Hagee's DVD gives an excellent understanding of the four blood moons. Pastor John Hagee is a great resource for other biblical topics as well. Some of Pastor Hagee's insights are mentioned herein.

Timeanddate.com has the dates of Jewish High Holy Days – Holidays, dating back in history through the current year.

Hal Lindsey, *The Late Great Planet Earth,* www.hallindsey.com. Hal Lindsey has been called the father of modern-day prophecy. There are some great insights that Mr. Lindsey included in *Late Great Planet Earth*, a few of which I referred to in chapters above.

Antony Flew, *There Is a God.* "How the world's most notorious atheist changed his mind." One of the most important factors that seem to have changed Mr. Flew's mind seems to be the Cosmological Fine Tuning. Mr. Flew writes in a way that most of us can understand.

Lee Strobel, *Case for a Creator.* Science and other apologetic "case points" for God. If you would like to have a general understanding of the Cosmological Fine Tuning and other insights, but you do not like deep science, this may be a book for you. Lee works to give a layman's view for those of us who do not understand the deep thoughts.

Josh McDowell, *More Than a Carpenter, Evidence That Demands a Verdict,* and other books, CDs, etc. Excellent apologetic proofs. McDowell investigates the historical record of Christ and the Bible.

Ravi Zacharias, *The Real Face of Atheism, Deliver Us from Evil.* Ravi is excellent in philosophical apologetics.

John Stott, *Basic Christianity.*

Blaise Pascal, *The Mind On Fire, Thoughts.* A brilliant mathematician from long ago gives very confident apologetic evidence for God and Christ. Some of his mathematical equations are still in use today. You can tell he was a genius by the way he can compress so much thought into one sentence.

Thomas V. Morris, *Making Sense of It All: Pascal and the Meaning of Life.* A look at the philosophical genius of Blaise Pascal. When the going gets tough attempting to understand Pascal, Morris helps us understand. An enjoyable read.

C. S. Lewis, *Mere Christianity, Surprised by Joy.* Excellent insight into the validity of Christianity.

Michael J. Behe, *Darwin's Black Box.* This book looks at the sophistication of some seemingly simple biological components, describing them as "irreducibly complex.

Endnotes

Chapter 3 Notes

1   Ross Hugh, *The Creator and the Cosmos* (Colorado Springs, CO: NavPress, 1993); Gerald L. Schroeder, *The Science of God* (New York: Free Press, 1997); Peter D. Ward and Donald Brownlee, *Rare Earth* (New York: Copernicus, 2000).

2   J. C. Sanford, *Genetic Entropy & The Mystery of the Genome* (Waterloo, NY: FMS, 2008).

3   Stephen C. Meyer, *Signature in the Cell* (New York: Harper One, 2009).

Chapter 5 Notes

1   Hal Lindsey noticed these concepts and mentioned them in his book *The Late Great Planet Earth*. "'We are told in Daniel 12 how prophecy "will not be understood until the end times, when travel and education shall be vastly increased.'" Hal Lindsey, *Late Great Planet Earth* (Grand Rapids, MI: Zondervan, 1970), 89. Also see The Hal Lindsey Report, www.hallindsey.com.

2   The Hal Lindsey Report, www.hallindseycom.

1   "20th Century Saw 65% of Christian Martyrs," EWTN news (www.ewtn. com/vnews/getstory.asp?number=26402). On modern persecution, see Dan Wooding, "More Christians Have Died for Their Faith in This Century Than All Other Centuries of Church History Combined," Christianity.com, www.Christianity/.com/church/church-history/timeline/1901-2000/modern-persecution-11630665.htm/. For some reason many of us have not seen this information in the news media.

Chapter 9 Note

1   For this country count and most facts cited in this chapter, I have relied on Wikipedia. See https://en.wikipedia.org/wiki/Main_Page.

Chapter 12 Notes

1   Thanks to Mark Blitz. See resources available from EL SHADDAI Ministries, www.elshaddaiministries.us.

2   The figures on blood moons and specific blood moon data were gleaned from Wikipedia's list of twenty-first-century lunar eclipses. Much more data is available.

Chapter 24 Note

1   Jonathan Cahn, *The Mystery of the Seventh Shemitah: The Mystery of the Shemitah VI,* DVD (Lodi, NJ: Hope of the World, 2013), DVD.

Printed in the United States
By Bookmasters